Instagram®
For Business

by Jenn Herman
Eric Butow
Corey Walker

for dummies®
A Wiley Brand

Instagram® For Business For Dummies®

Published by: **John Wiley & Sons, Inc.,** 111 River Street, Hoboken, NJ 07030-5774, www.wiley.com

Copyright © 2018 by John Wiley & Sons, Inc., Hoboken, New Jersey

Published simultaneously in Canada

No part of this publication may be reproduced, stored in a retrieval system or transmitted in any form or by any means, electronic, mechanical, photocopying, recording, scanning or otherwise, except as permitted under Sections 107 or 108 of the 1976 United States Copyright Act, without the prior written permission of the Publisher. Requests to the Publisher for permission should be addressed to the Permissions Department, John Wiley & Sons, Inc., 111 River Street, Hoboken, NJ 07030, (201) 748-6011, fax (201) 748-6008, or online at http://www.wiley.com/go/permissions.

Trademarks: Wiley, For Dummies, the Dummies Man logo, Dummies.com, Making Everything Easier, and related trade dress are trademarks or registered trademarks of John Wiley & Sons, Inc. and may not be used without written permission. Instagram is a registered trademark of Instagram, LLC. All other trademarks are the property of their respective owners. John Wiley & Sons, Inc. is not associated with any product or vendor mentioned in this book.

For general information on our other products and services, please contact our Customer Care Department within the U.S. at 877-762-2974, outside the U.S. at 317-572-3993, or fax 317-572-4002. For technical support, please visit https://hub.wiley.com/community/support/dummies.

Wiley publishes in a variety of print and electronic formats and by print-on-demand. Some material included with standard print versions of this book may not be included in e-books or in print-on-demand. If this book refers to media such as a CD or DVD that is not included in the version you purchased, you may download this material at http://booksupport.wiley.com. For more information about Wiley products, visit www.wiley.com.

Library of Congress Control Number: 2017960436

ISBN 978-1-119-43981-3 (pbk); ISBN 978-1-119-43980-6 (ebk); ISBN 978-1-119-43984-4 (ebk)

Manufactured in the United States of America

10 9 8 7 6 5 4 3 2 1

Contents at a Glance

Table of Contents

Introduction

Are you ready to have some fun? We hope you are! Because Instagram is all about entertainment and creating exciting content. Because you've chosen this book, we know you're ready to get down to business to create an Instagram account that will not only help you grow your business but also be something you enjoy!

With more and more people joining Instagram every day, the social media app continues to grow at unprecedented rates. But with that growth comes a lot of noise and saturation from people who don't quite understand how to use the platform effectively. After reading this book, however, you'll have the tools and tactics necessary to build a successful Instagram profile.

About This Book

The purpose of *Instagram For Business For Dummies* is simply to help you use Instagram effectively. As you can see by the number of pages in this book, that purpose is easier said than done! In fact, some people think that Instagram marketing means just uploading a photo to Instagram.

Instagram really is as simple as uploading a photo. But for strategic business use, you should employ a number of marketing and traffic-generating tactics, which we explore in this book. And as Instagram adds more features to the platform, such as multi-image posts and Instagram Stories, understanding how to create this additional content is just as important.

We take you through every step of creating and uploading content to Instagram, writing effective captions that get your audience to take action, finding hashtags that help you get more exposure, building your audience, and using all the fun features built into Instagram.

Foolish Assumptions

When writing this book, we assumed that you

>> Have a business or are getting ready to start a business

>> Have a website for your business

>> Know your target customer audience and know that they're using Instagram

>> Want to use Instagram effectively to drive real business results

>> Don't want to look like an amateur, even if you're new to using Instagram

>> Are committed to devoting time and energy to build a presence on Instagram that will reflect your brand

Instagram is an interactive and community-focused platform. We hope that you understand this and are looking forward to building a community around your brand.

If these assumptions are correct, this is the right book for you! We're confident that the tactics and information here will help you achieve your goals.

Icons Used in This Book

To make things easier and ensure that you don't miss important details, we have various icons throughout this book. Here's what the different icons look like and mean.

TIP

The Tip icon is a small piece of expert advice that will save you time and make your experience on Instagram easier to master.

REMEMBER

Because we cover a lot of details and information, every now and then we throw in a Remember icon to remind you of important details we've already covered. We know you're reading every juicy detail of the book; the Remember icon just helps resurface some of those tidbits.

TECHNICAL STUFF

Who doesn't love a little geek-fest on technical jargon? Okay, a lot of people! But that's why we've pulled out these paragraphs so that you can understand the technical aspects of using Instagram without getting overwhelmed.

WARNING

Yes, this book has a few warnings. When you see a Warning icon, please take a few extra moments to understand the effect of what we're saying. You're not going to blow up your Instagram account or do anything irreparable, but we want to save you from any headaches we can.

Beyond the Book

In addition to what you're reading right now, this book also comes with a free, access-anywhere cheat sheet that provides a handy list of Instagram lingo, steps for sharing posts directly, and more. To view the cheat sheet, simply go to www.dummies.com and type **Instagram for Business For Dummies Cheat Sheet** in the Search box.

Where to Go from Here

The first few chapters dive into how to set up a new Instagram account. If you already have an Instagram account, you can skip the first chapter, but we encourage you to check out Chapter 2 because it contains information on how to set up an effective profile. Don't worry, you can easily update or edit anything you've already started!

After that, we have a ton of information on creating better content and getting strategic with your Instagram content. If you want to focus on specific areas, look at the Table of Contents for guidance.

If you run into trouble, check out Chapters 15 and 16, which are dedicated to troubleshooting Instagram issues. And if you are looking for inspiration, read Chapters 17 and 18.

It's time to jump into all the fun of Instagram that we've been talking about! Enjoy the book.

1

Creating Your Profile

Install Instagram on your smartphone, tablet, or Windows computer.

Set up your Instagram business profile to draw followers like moths to a flame (or whatever trite saying applies).

Prepare your business goals for your Instagram profile so you can reach the most customers.

Chapter **1**

Installing Instagram

The good people at the Instagram division of Facebook realized long ago that many people use Instagram with all their computing devices, not just smartphones. What's more, they knew that if business owners were going to adopt Instagram as the de facto photo-sharing app, Instagram had to be available everywhere: on smartphones, tablets, computers, and even the Instagram website.

If you haven't installed Instagram yet, this is the chapter you need to read. We start by showing you where to find Instagram on the web, and then you find out how to install the Instagram app on computers, smartphones, and tablets.

Next, you see how to use Instagram on the web in case you're using a computer or device that either doesn't or can't have Instagram installed, such as a company smartphone that allows only company-approved apps. Finally, you launch the Instagram app on your computer or device so you can scratch that itch and start Instagramming.

Moving Instagram to the Launch Pad

Facebook had the good sense to keep the Instagram website intact, so you don't have to go through the Facebook website to get to all that Instagram goodness. As soon as you type *www.instagram.com* in your browser and press Enter (or Return), the Instagram website kindly checks your computer to see whether it has Instagram installed.

TIP

If the website reports that it's having trouble checking your system for Instagram, you need to enable cookies in your web browser settings. After you enable cookies, refresh the Instagram website page and it will check your system.

If you don't have Instagram installed, you'll see a brightly colored bar at the top of the page, where Instagram (having detected the operating system you're using) invites you to visit the applicable app store to download the latest version, such as the Windows example shown in Figure 1-1.

FIGURE 1-1:
Get the Windows
Instagram app
by clicking Get at
the top right.

So what happens if Instagram finds that the app is installed? If you're using Windows or a Mac, the app screen will appear in a new window or tab. On your smartphone or tablet, the app opens and appears on your screen.

REMEMBER

If your workplace has a BYOD (Bring Your Own Device) policy, pass this book around to the people in your company so they can refer to the appropriate section in this chapter for installing Instagram on their computer or device.

Installing on a Computer

Instagram was designed for a smartphone, but in a business setting you'll be more likely to view it at your desk while you're working. Otherwise, you'll have to keep looking from your computer screen to your smartphone.

Fortunately, the Instagram app is available for Windows and the Mac, so you can view, like, and comment on photos and videos from other Instagram users. However, you can't use your computer's webcam to take pictures or shoot video.

TIP

Feel free to skip ahead to the "No App? No Problem: Instagram Is on the Web" section to learn how to use the Instagram website. (This information should go in your brain's "be prepared" file.) Then continue reading to the end of the chapter to learn how to log in to Instagram.

Installing on a Windows PC (sort of)

The Windows version of Instagram is a Windows 10 app. As any Windows 10 user knows, Microsoft is trying to make Windows the best of both worlds by offering apps that can run on both Windows on computers and the Windows Mobile 10 operating system. (Good luck trying to find anyone using Windows Mobile 10 on a smartphone.)

Windows PC users can install the Instagram app from the Windows Store or the Instagram website. Here's how to install the app from the Windows Store:

1. **Click the Start icon in the taskbar.**

2. **Click Store in the list of programs or click the Start tile in the Start menu.**

3. **In the Search box, type** Instagram.

4. **In the list that appears below the Search box, click Instagram.**

5. **Click the Install button, as shown in Figure 1-2.**

After the Windows Store installs the Instagram app on your computer, the Install button in the Store window changes to Launch.

6. **Click Launch to start the app.**

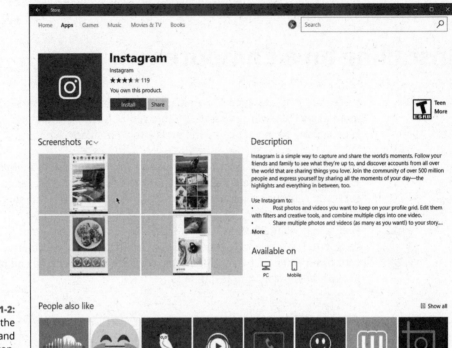

FIGURE 1-2:
Click Install to the right of the bland Instagram icon.

If you prefer to install the Windows app from the Instagram website, follow these steps:

1. **Navigate to the Instagram website.**

2. **Click the Get button in the upper-right corner of the Instagram web page.**

The Store window appears in front of your browser window.

3. **Click the Install button (refer to Figure 1-2).**

4. **After installation, start the app by clicking the Launch button.**

Now you can skip ahead of the rest of the class and start Instagramming by going to the "Starting to Gram Instantly" section.

Installing on a Mac (sort of)

Instagram doesn't have a Mac version of its app available to download, as you'll discover if you search for Instagram in the App Store. If you try to download the app from iTunes by clicking Get on the Instagram app page, you'll see the Get button change to Downloading for a few seconds, and then the button will change back to Get.

The only way you can access Instagram is on its website. And if you use a web browser other than Safari, you'll only be able to view, like, and comment on photos and videos. Fortunately, you can bamboozle the Instagram website into thinking you're accessing the website on the iPhone so you can upload photos.

REMEMBER

You can only upload photos from your Mac from the bamboozled Instagram website. You can't take photos, shoot videos, or upload videos.

An article by Lewis Painter on the Macworld UK website (`www.macworld.co.uk/how-to/mac-software/how-use-instagram-on-mac-2017-3641569/`) tells you how to do this. But rather than make you go to the website for this information, we tell you how here:

1. **Open Safari.**

2. **Choose Safari ⇨ Preferences or press Command+, (comma).**

3. **Click the Show Develop Menu in Menu Bar check box, shown at the bottom of Figure 1-3.**

4. **Close the window.**

    The Develop option now appears in the menu bar.

5. **Click Develop, move the mouse pointer over User Agent, and then click Safari—iOS 10—iPhone in the side menu.**

6. **Open the Instagram website and log in.**

    The Instagram home screen appears, as shown in Figure 1-4.

7. **Click the camera icon.**

    The File window opens so you can navigate to your desired folder and add photo(s) to your Instagram profile.

WARNING

If you click the Open in App button (above the camera icon, as shown in Figure 1-4), Safari will tell you that it can't open the specified address. Close this button by clicking the X in the button.

FIGURE 1-3:
Display the
Develop menu in
the Safari menu
bar by clicking
the check box at
the bottom.

FIGURE 1-4:
To upload a
photo, click the
camera icon.

Alas and alack, after you upload your photos, you'll find that the photo-editing options in Safari are more limited than those in the iPhone app. (And remember that you can't upload videos to Instagram on Safari.)

If you'd rather upload photos to Instagram by using an app, check out the two apps that the Instagram website lists: Flume and Uplet. A discussion of third-party apps is beyond the scope of this book, so please visit the website for that information.

Now that you have Instagram doing your bidding on your Mac, start using Instagram by moving ahead to the "Starting to Gram Instantly" section.

Installing on Instagram's Native Platform

The first version of Instagram, which was available for download on October 6, 2010, was for iPhone users. It was a wise decision: The popularity of the iPhone combined with Instagram's ease of use when it came to sharing photos resulted in more than one million registered Instagram users by the end of 2010. You can install the iPhone app not only on your iPhone but also on your iPad if you prefer to use your tablet.

Installing on an iPhone

It's easy to download Instagram from the App Store to your iPhone:

1. **Tap the App Store icon.**

2. **Tap the magnifying glass icon at the bottom of the screen.**

3. **Tap the Search icon in the lower-right corner of the screen.**

4. **Tap the Search box, at the top of the screen, and start typing the word** Instagram.

   After you type the first few letters, Instagram appears at the top of the results list.

5. **Tap Instagram in the results list.**

   The app information appears on the screen, as shown in Figure 1-5.

6. **Tap Get.**

   If you need to sign into the App Store, type your password in the Sign In to iTunes Store window and then tap Buy. (If you use Touch ID instead of typing your password, place the appropriate finger or thumb on the Home button.)

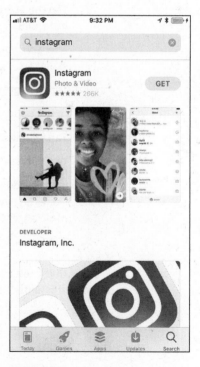

FIGURE 1-5:
The Instagram app on an iPhone.

7. **Tap Open.**

The next time you want to open Instagram, swipe to the Home screen that has room for icons — because that's where you'll find the Instagram icon.

Now Instagram is ready for you to start using it, so move ahead to the "Starting to Gram Instantly" section.

Installing on an iPad

Instagram has yet to create a native app for the iPad, which is another one of life's great mysteries (but not at the level of where missing socks go). However, you can use the iPhone app on the iPad.

Here's how to install Instagram on an iPad:

1. **Tap the App Store icon.**

2. **Tap the Search icon in the lower-right corner of the screen.**

3. **Tap the Search box, at the top of the screen, and start typing the word** Instagram.

   After you type the first two or three letters, Instagram appears at the top of the results list.

4. **Tap Instagram in the results list.**

5. **In the upper-left corner of the screen, tap Supports.**

6. **Tap iPhone Only, as shown in Figure 1-6.**

7. **Tap Get (see Figure 1-7).**

   If you need to sign into the App Store, type your password in the Sign In to iTunes Store window. Then tap Buy. Or, if you use Touch ID, place the appropriate finger or thumb on the Home button instead.

8. **Tap Open.**

Now that you've installed Instagram on your iPad, go straight to the "Starting to Gram Instantly" section to learn how to start using Instagram.

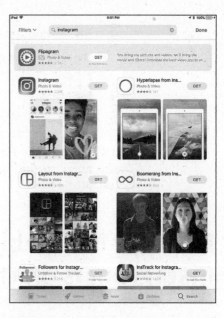

FIGURE 1-6:
Yes, tap iPhone only when you're installing Instagram on your iPad.

FIGURE 1-7:
The Instagram app is in the upper-left corner.

Instagram Has Android Covered, Too

After Instagram was satisfied with the development of its app on the iPhone, staffers turned their attention to developing Instagram for the Android platform. On the first day the app was released, in April 2012, more than a million users downloaded it.

Here's how to install Instagram from the Google Play Store:

1. **Tap the Play Store icon on the Home screen.**

   If the Play Store icon isn't on a Home screen, tap Apps on the Home screen and then tap Play Store in the Apps screen.

2. **Tap the Search box at the top of the screen, and start typing the word** Instagram**.**

   After you type, Instagram appears in the results list.

3. **Tap Instagram in the results list.**

   The app information screen shown in Figure 1-8 appears.

4. **Tap Install.**

5. **Tap Open.**

It's time to start Instagramming, so skip ahead to the "Starting to Gram Instantly" section.

No App? No Problem: Instagram Is on the Web

If your company doesn't allow you to install unauthorized apps on company smartphones, you can still access the Instagram website on your smartphone or computer, but there is less functionality.

Open the Instagram website by typing *www.instagram.com* in your browser's address bar. You can log in to Instagram on the web in one of two ways:

>> **Instagram username and password:** Type your Instagram username in the Username box and then type your password in the Password box. Then click or tap Log In.

>> **Facebook account:** If you prefer to use your Facebook account, click or tap Log In with Facebook. (If your browser doesn't have your Facebook account information stored in a cookie, the Facebook window appears on your screen so you can type your username and password.) Then click or tap the Log In As button.

REMEMBER

If you haven't created an Instagram account yet, bookmark this page and read Chapter 2 to learn how to create an effective profile.

After you log in, you see the home page with the latest photos and videos from users you follow. The top of the screen, shown in Figure 1-9, features the Instagram logo at the left, the Search box in the center, and three icons to the right of the Search box:

- » **Compass icon:** Opens the Discover People page so you can view a list of other users whom Instagram thinks you may want to follow. To follow a user, click the Follow button.

- » **Heart icon:** Displays a list of notifications, such as when someone comments on one of your photos or videos.

- » **Person icon:** Displays your Profile page.

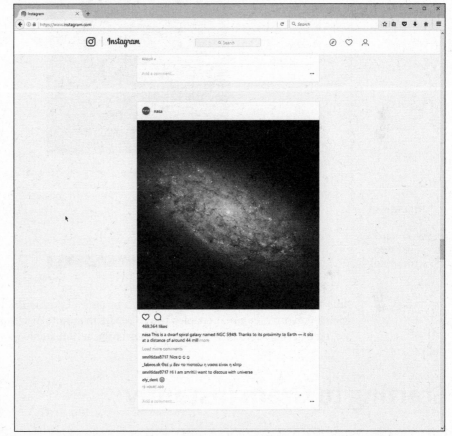

FIGURE 1-9:
The Search box is at the top of the page.

If you're on the Discover People or Profile pages, you can return to the home page by clicking the Instagram icon (camera) or the Instagram logo.

Scroll down the screen to see photos and videos from other Instagram users you follow. Below the photo, you can click the heart icon to like the photo. You can also add a comment by clicking Add a Comment (see Figure 1-10), typing the comment, and then pressing Enter.

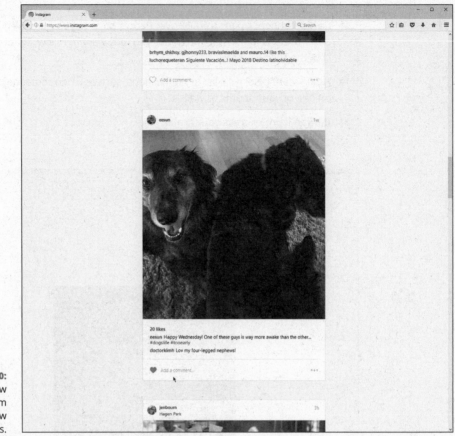

FIGURE 1-10:
You can view
comments from
other users below
the photos.

Note the icon with three dots to the right of Add a Comment. Click this icon to open a pop-up menu that enables you to report the photo or video as inappropriate, embed the photo on a website, or cancel the action and close the menu.

Starting to Gram Instantly

If you've installed the Instagram app on your Windows PC or smartphone, you should use those versions instead of the tablet versions or the website because they have more functionality. And if you have a choice between using a PC or a smartphone, remember that iPhone and Android smartphone versions of Instagram have the most functionality of all.

REMEMBER

You can also use the smartphone version of the Instagram app on your iPad or Android tablet.

Starting Instagram on a computer

To open Instagram on your Windows PC, click the Start icon in the taskbar and then click Instagram in the apps list, as shown in Figure 1-11. Alternatively, you can click the Instagram icon in the Start menu.

FIGURE 1-11: The Instagram app is in the I section of the apps list.

After you launch the app for the first time, it will ask you to sign in using your Instagram username and password or to log in with your Facebook account.

If you don't have an Instagram account, click the Sign Up link at the bottom of the window. The signup screen asks you to log in with Facebook or create an Instagram account by clicking the Sign Up with Phone or Email link. From there, you'll be able to use the signup wizard to create an account.

TIP

Want to launch Instagram from your taskbar? Simply right-click the Instagram icon in the taskbar, and click Pin to Taskbar.

Starting Instagram on a mobile device

If you're using Instagram on an iPhone, iPad, or Android device, you can start the app by tapping its icon, as shown in Figure 1-12.

If you're using Instagram on an iPhone or iPad, you'll be asked to turn on Instagram notifications in the Please Turn On Notifications window. If you don't turn them on, you won't know, for example, if one of your followers likes a photo you posted. Turn on Instagram notifications by tapping OK in the window. Next, you see the Instagram Would Like to Send You Notifications window. This seems redundant, but Instagram is asking you to send your notifications with sounds and alerts. If you want to do this, tap Allow in the window. Otherwise, tap Don't Allow in the window.

If you're using an Android smartphone or tablet, you won't see a notification window. Instead, you'll see your home screen. You can change the notification settings in Instagram for Android, as you discover in Chapter 15.

FIGURE 1-12:
The Instagram icon appears in the third row of icons on this iPhone.

Chapter **2**

Setting Up Your Profile

After you install the Instagram app on your mobile device, the first major task you face is setting up your profile. Your profile should accurately represent your business brand — and appeal to your target audience.

In this chapter, we show you how to set up the different components of your profile. Although a profile has several components, establishing the right username immediately is the most important. Proper selection at the beginning ensures that you don't have to make unwanted changes in the future or compensate for an irrelevant username as your business grows. If you set up your Instagram profile foundations to align with your brand, you'll be able to edit additional components as you grow and better drive business results from your Instagram account.

Professional Profile Practices

Your *Instagram profile* is both your first impression to potential customers and new visitors as well as your consistent branded message to your existing audience. Your profile should be recognizable to your audience and showcase the value you provide as a business. See Figure 2-1.

Instagram profiles are comprised of the following six components: username, profile photo, name, bio, website URL, and business address (optional). In addition, profiles that have upgraded to a business account have contact buttons. We talk more about all these elements in the coming sections.

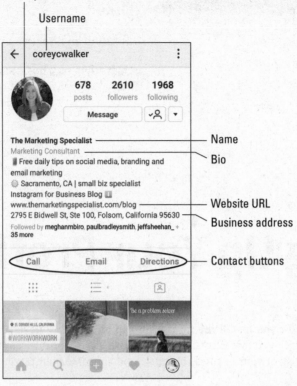

Profile photo

Username

Name

Bio

Website URL

Business address

Contact buttons

FIGURE 2-1:
The Instagram profile consists of these standard components.

Your profile should be consistent with the branding and messaging you use on other online marketing platforms, but it should also align with the styling and formatting that appeals to Instagram users. Note too that you need to format your profile according to Instagram's formatting and character restrictions. These limits and restrictions are discussed in more detail later in this chapter.

Choosing a name and username for your business

Your name and username are two of the most important components of your Instagram profile because they are the only two searchable criteria of your profile. When users type a keyword or name in the search field on Instagram, the app looks at only the username and name fields of accounts to determine if an account is relevant to that search query.

REMEMBER

The username is the string of characters at the top of profile. The name is the bold text below the profile photo. If you want your business to be found by a keyword or phrase, be sure to include it in either the name or username for your account.

Choosing the best username

You must select a username when you set up a new Instagram account. Your *Instagram username* is how you are recognized on Instagram: All activity, from the content you post to how you engage with others, is associated with your username. The username is at the top of the profile, as shown in Figure 2-2.

Your username is the component of your Instagram URL that defines your account. It's delineated with the @ symbol when referring to you as a user. The URL for your Instagram account is

```
http://instagram.com/yourusername
```

When you interact on Instagram, the username appears as

yourusername

An Instagram username is limited to 30 characters and must contain only letters, numbers, periods, and underscores. You can't include symbols or other punctuation marks as a part of your username.

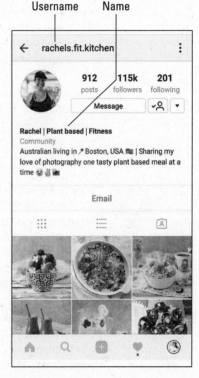

FIGURE 2-2:
The username of your account is listed at the top of your profile.

Choose a username that represents your brand, is recognizable, and, if possible, distinguishes what you do. Your username might be simply your business name or an adapted version of your business name, such as @louboutinworld, instead of Christian Louboutin. Or you might also include a word or two that describes your business industry or niche to further define who you are, such as @yorkelee_prints.

TIP

Choosing a username that is different than your business name may confuse Instagram users as to whether or not your account is the official account for your business. It's best to keep variations as minimal as possible to avoid confusion.

During the registration portion of your Instagram account, you're prompted to select your username. If the username you selected is available, a check mark will appear. If someone is using that username, an X will appear in the username field. Keep selecting alternatives until you find an available username.

Usernames are provided on a first-come basis. If you're signing up for a new Instagram account using the web version, Instagram will populate an available username for you. Delete this username and type one that represents your brand. If the username you want to use is unavailable, you can use alternative options by adding periods or underscores to the username, by using abbreviations, or by adding another word.

There is little you can do to have an existing username transferred to your account if it's in use or was previously used by another account. If another account is using your registered trademark as its username, visit https://help.instagram.com/101826856646059 for information on how to file a claim of trademark violation.

TIP

It's good practice to read your username objectively before finalizing it. When you combine more than one word into a single username, without spacing, the arrangement of the letters may read differently or inappropriately to others. For example, @yourusername might be read as "You Ruse R Name" instead of "Your Username." When this is the case, consider adding periods or underscores to separate the words within the username as follows: @your.username or @your_username.

After you select a username, all content linking to your profile is associated with the username's URL. If you want to change the username at some point, your URL would change and you would need to update all backlinks and links to that profile accordingly. This is why it's best to choose the right username when setting up your profile.

If you do want to change your username, follow these easy steps:

1. **Go to your profile on Instagram on either your mobile device or your computer.**

2. **Tap or click Edit Profile.**

3. **In the Username field, type the new username.**

4. **Save your changes.**

   To do so, tap the check mark, Done, Save, or Submit button (depending on the device you're using).

Choosing the best name

Your *Instagram name* is visible only when someone visits your profile directly. The name appears in bold below the profile photo (refer to Figure 2-2).

Your profile will perform better in searches and look more professional if the name and username are different. Having a name that's different from your username provides double the opportunity for keywords and searchable criteria in the Instagram app. Power users on Instagram take the time to craft good username and name components.

Unlike your username, which is one word, your name should be in proper sentence structure with capital letters and spacing. Your name (like your username) is limited to 30 characters, including spaces.

You can use your actual name or business name as your name on Instagram. Or you may choose to use an abbreviation or a commonly recognized description of your business. For example, if your business is a pizza restaurant called Farm Fresh Pizza, your username might be farm.fresh.pizza and your name might be Best Pizzeria in Boston.

TIP

You can be found in more searches on Instagram if you include a keyword or phrase in your name or username or both. If you didn't put a defining keyword in your username, you should include one in your name field, in addition to your actual name. For example, in Figure 2-2, Rachel added the keywords *Plant Based* and *Fitness* to her name field.

The name on your profile is not tied to your URL or other defining aspects of Instagram, so you can change it at any time. Consider adding or changing keywords, as necessary, to appeal to your target audience on Instagram.

If you want to change your name, do the following:

1. **Go to your Instagram profile, and tap or click Edit Profile.**

2. **In the Name field, type the new name.**

3. **Save your changes.**

   To do so, tap the check mark, Done, Save, or Submit button (depending on the device you're using).

Choosing a profile photo that attracts customers

The *profile photo* on your account, as well as your username, is associated with all your activity. When you post anything to Instagram or engage with other users in any way, your profile photo is visible.

Your profile photo should represent your brand and be recognizable to others. If your company is actively using other social media platforms, its Instagram profile photo should be the same as the one used on other platforms. In this way, you create cohesion across your online media and assure your customers that they found the correct account when searching for you.

TIP

Profile photos on Instagram are cropped to a circle, so your photo should fit properly within that crop. Don't use a logo or an image that loses valuable content when cropped to a circle.

The profile photo on your profile page appears larger than anywhere else on Instagram. When interacting with others, the profile photo is a thumbnail (small) version. Choose an image that isn't too busy, overwhelming, or cluttered with text, because the image will become difficult to decipher as a thumbnail.

The best profile photos are high resolution so that they have a clear object of focus, contain a simple background, and don't pixelate. (In a *pixelated* photo, a low-resolution image is enlarged too much and the individual square pixels become obvious, making the image blurry.)

Writing a Bio That Draws in Followers

Your *Instagram bio* is a short description on your profile that tells people about your business. This description is similar to a 30-second elevator speech and is how you convince new visitors to follow your account.

Most people will read your bio only the first time they visit your profile. Your bio is the first impression you give to new viewers and should accurately convey the message you want to share.

Deciding what information to include

Before you start writing your bio, choose at least two or three key aspects of your business to highlight. These should be traits that will connect emotionally, in some way, with your ideal target audience, such as the examples shown in Figure 2-3.

You also need to determine the voice and style of your bio. If your brand is known for being humorous and witty, your Instagram bio should reflect that same style through words and relevant emojis. In contrast, if your brand is professional and classy, your bio should not be silly and humorous.

FIGURE 2-3:
Effective Instagram bios immediately convey value to the visitor.

To market effectively on Instagram, you must know your target audience and how they're using Instagram. Your bio should be written in a way that connects with the people in that specific demographic. Determine the characteristics that you most want to connect with in that audience and write your bio accordingly. For example, in Figure 2-4, the target audience is people who want to learn about video marketing and how to create their own videos. The bio is written to appeal to that audience.

The Instagram bio is limited to 150 characters, including spaces. The bio is designed to be one single paragraph of information, but you can use formatting techniques to add spaces and line breaks.

TIP

Because Instagram was designed to be used on a mobile device, it's best to format your bio on a mobile device so that you retain the correct formatting and alignment. No matter what formatting you create, your bio on a desktop or computer device will always be one long paragraph spanning the width of the browser, unlike the vertical alignment seen on mobile devices.

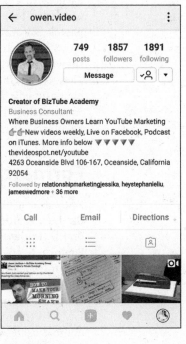

FIGURE 2-4:
The Instagram bio for @owen.video is designed to appeal to people interested in video marketing.

Include the emojis and symbols on your device's keyboard in your bio to create visual appeal and to better connect with your audience. To add emojis, you must open the emoji keyboard on your mobile device. An iOS user should tap the smiley face icon at the bottom of the keyboard. An Android user can tap the smiley face button to the left of the spacebar. (If you don't see a smiley face, tap and hold down on the microphone icon to display a pop-up menu, where you can select the smiley face icon.) Instagram is a visual platform, and having icons in the bio helps yours stand out from others. You have many emojis to choose from. If the traditional funny face and cartoonish emojis don't translate to your brand's style, use simple emoji symbols such as squares, diamonds, triangles, and arrows to add color and visual content without detracting from your professional style.

Hashtags aren't clickable in the Instagram bio on mobile devices, so including a hashtag in your bio description is irrelevant. The exception is if you have a unique branded hashtag that you want people to associate with your brand. For example, @sandiego photos encourages followers to use the #MySDPhoto hashtag to have their photos showcased on their account (see Figure 2-5). They use this for branding purposes, because the hashtag is still not clickable. We talk all about using hashtags on Instagram in Chapter 8.

Formatting your bio

You can edit or create your bio by tapping the Edit Profile button in your Instagram profile. In the Edit Profile screen, shown in Figure 2-6, go to the Bio field and insert the text for your bio. Save any changes when you're finished. Please note that Figure 2-6 shows the setup for a business profile.

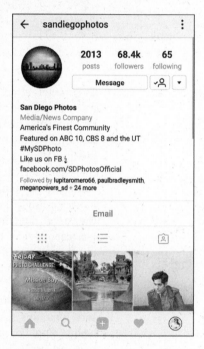

FIGURE 2-5:
A hashtag in your Instagram bio can be helpful for branding but is not clickable.

Android users can format a bio completely in Instagram. If you want to include line breaks and spacing, tap the Return or Enter key (on the keyboard of your mobile device) at the end of the line. Make sure that you don't have an extra space after the final character on the line and that the last character on the line is not an emoji. Otherwise, the breaks you inserted with the Return or Enter key will not appear in your published text.

iOS users can format a bio in Instagram, but line breaks will not be retained. Instead, it's best to open a note app on your device and use it to craft your bio description, including all formatting. Then copy the bio, open Instagram again, select Edit Profile, and paste the description in the Bio field. As with Android users, you must ensure that no extra space appears after the final character on the line and that the last character on the line is not an emoji.

TIP

Your bio can be edited and rewritten as often as you want. It's a best practice to review your bio every six months and verify that the information is still accurate and relevant. If something should be revised, go through the editing steps used to set up your initial bio to change the text.

If you run marketing campaigns or have seasonal content or promotions, you can update your bio to align with these events.

FIGURE 2-6:
Add your bio in the Edit Profile screen.

Using a call to action to drive website traffic

The last line of your bio should be a call to action (CTA) that directs visitors to click the URL listed below it. (We cover this URL setup in the next section.) The call to action should be clear and actionable but also specific to the action you're asking visitors to do.

Do not simply write *Visit our website* or *Click below*. Instead, use something like *Get your free ebook here* or *Shop our new styles now*. Include a down-arrow emoji at the end of the CTA that points to where the URL will appear in the bio (refer to the examples in Figure 2-3).

As with the rest of your bio, the CTA can be edited as often as you like. Experiment with different wording to determine which drives the best number of clicks to your website.

Choosing a website link that encourages clicks

The most effective way to generate website traffic from Instagram is to use the only clickable URL on the platform — the link in your bio.

You can maximize your website traffic by ensuring that the URL in your bio takes visitors to the exact page you're promoting. For example, if you're promoting an opportunity to sign up for your newsletter but the link goes to your website home page where there's no place to sign up, you'll lose potential registrants. In this case, you want the link to go directly to the website page where the signup form is located, making it easy for your Instagram audience to sign up quickly.

Your URL can be updated or changed as frequently as you like. You might have a default web page for your profile but change it to coincide with a promotion or campaign you're running on Instagram. After that campaign is complete, you can change the link back to your default.

TECHNICAL STUFF

To accurately track your Instagram traffic, you need to do more than upload a direct link to your website. If someone clicks the link in your bio from Instagram on the desktop, Google Analytics records it as referral traffic from Instagram. When someone taps the link in Instagram on a mobile device, a new browser is opened. Google Analytics doesn't properly track that traffic for you. Instead, it considers opening the new browser *direct* traffic, not social media referral traffic.

Although Google Analytics is tracking that traffic for you, it's categorizing it alongside all other direct traffic to your site, not as a click-through from Instagram. As a result, you may look at your website traffic and be convinced that Instagram is not driving any significant traffic, when it may be sending much more traffic than you're aware of.

To correct this, use a link shortener that provides trackable data on the number of clicks. The link shorteners Bitly, goo.gl, and Rebrandly are the most reliable and safe options. Each provides a data analysis of each link to allow you to track how many clicks you're generating.

To use a link shortener, follow these simple steps:

1. **Find your long-form URL (the direct link from your website) and copy it.**

2. **Open the link shortener website of your choice.**

3. **Paste the long-form URL in the link shortener website.**

    The link shortener generates a short link.

4. Customize the short URL to match your branding or page.

5. Copy the short URL and paste it as your URL in your Instagram bio.

TIP

Most link shorteners generate a link with random letters and numbers, such as `http://bit.ly/2X4y6`. This doesn't look professional, and visitors might find the link confusing or might question the link's validity. You can simply customize the link to reflect your brand. For example, if your long-form URL is `http://jennstrends.com/blog`, the short-form one might be `http://bit.ly/JTBlog` or `http://bit.ly/JennsTrendsBlog`.

Taking Advantage of a Business Profile Upgrade

In late 2016, Instagram introduced business profiles to Instagram. Before this feature rolled out, all profiles on Instagram looked identical. Now brands have the capability to stand out from regular accounts and can benefit from a variety of features available only to business profiles.

By upgrading to a business profile on Instagram, you get features such as the following:

>> Easy-to-access contact buttons that make it easy for your customers to email you, call you, or get directions to your location

>> An industry listing that informs visitors what you do as a business

>> In-app analytics to best monitor what is and isn't working in your content strategy

>> The ability to boost posts from your Instagram profile and run ads on Instagram

>> The ability to manage your Instagram comments and engagement through your Facebook page

TIP

As mentioned, you are allowed only one clickable link (in your bio). The contact button feature means people can call or email you, providing you additional ways to connect directly with your customers and close more sales!

To upgrade to a business profile on Instagram, you must have a Facebook business page to which you can connect. Instagram advertising is managed through the Facebook Business Manager, and even if you don't plan to run ads, Instagram requires you to connect to a Facebook business page.

WARNING

You can connect only one Facebook page to one Instagram profile. If you manage multiple Instagram accounts and want to upgrade them all, they must each connect to a separate Facebook page.

Now that you've set up your Instagram account, as outlined in this chapter, you can easily upgrade your account to a business profile, following a few steps outlined next.

Connecting to a Facebook page

As mentioned, you need to have a Facebook business page if you want to upgrade to an Instagram business profile. Then you follow a few easy steps to connect your Instagram account to your Facebook business page and set up your contact information.

To upgrade your Instagram account to a business account, do the following:

1. **Log in to Instagram on your mobile device, and tap Edit Profile.**

   The Edit Profile screen appears, as shown in Figure 2-7.

2. **Select the Upgrade to Business Profile option or the Try Instagram Business Tools option.**

3. **Tap your way through the screens that highlight the value of business profiles.**

4. **When prompted, tap Continue to connect to a Facebook page.**

5. **Select your Facebook page.**

   If you manage only one Facebook page, that page is selected automatically. If you manage multiple Facebook pages, they will appear in the list of options. Select the page to which you want to connect.

   Information from your Facebook page, including your email address, phone number, and location, is imported, as shown in Figure 2-8.

   The contact info uploaded to the Instagram setup screen determines which contact buttons (Email, Phone, and Directions) appear on your profile. For example, if you don't include a phone number, the Call Contact button will not appear.

6. **Update or add information as necessary.**

   For example, if your information does not populate a phone number but you would like to include the *Call* contact button, you can add your phone number to that field in the Contact Options screen.

   You can edit this information at any time, in case you want to add or delete a contact option later.

FIGURE 2-7:
The Edit Profile screen has an option for upgrading to a business profile.

FIGURE 2-8:
Edit your contact information to populate the contact buttons on your profile.

7. **Save your information.**

   Tap the check mark in the top-right corner of the Contact Options screen.

Your Instagram account is now set up as a business profile!

Navigating your business profile

Now that you've upgraded to a business profile, you'll see some new features on your profile, as shown in Figure 2-9.

Business profile features allow you to make the most out of your Instagram account by tracking your account analytics, promoting your posts, and providing information to your audience about how to contact you:

>> The bar graph (in the top-right corner) is where you'll find your profile analytics. As you post content and build your audience, new information will be recorded in your analytics.

>> The Promote button allows you to create a paid advertising campaign based on content in your profile.

>> The industry tag associated with your Facebook page transfers over to your Instagram account and is listed in gray below your name.

>> The contact buttons you set up when upgrading your account appear on your profile, making it easy for your audience to contact you. (An Email contact button appears in Figure 2-9.)

After upgrading your account, your new business profile appears to people visiting your profile. If they're following you, they can tap the Message button to message you (via direct message) from your profile. They also see your contact buttons and industry listing. Figure 2-10 shows how a business profile looks to others.

Even though you have these additional features as a business profile, your profile characteristics, such as your username, name, bio, and URL, remain the same.

FIGURE 2-9:
Business profiles provide features not available to a regular Instagram account.

FIGURE 2-10:
Instagram users view your business profile with these added features.

» Researching your competition for
ideas for posts

» Choosing the best scheduling and
analytics platforms for your business
needs

Chapter **3**

Hitting Your Target Audience

You can take fabulous photos and create cute graphics to promote your business on Instagram all day long, but putting a plan in place is crucial for true success. If it seems like there's no rhyme or reason to the posts from some businesses, it's because there isn't. But you are different. You want to do it right, which is why you're reading this book.

In this chapter, you start by determining your business goals and deciding whether you need a team to fulfill them. Then you find out how to gather post ideas by researching your competition, figuring out post types, and putting your content into an organized content schedule. Finally, the chapter gets more techie, showing you how to schedule and analyze your posts to save time and create a more successful campaign.

Organizing Your Marketing Goals and Roles

Before you dive deeply into how to take the perfect Insta-awesome photo, you should establish your business goals for the account. Instagram is a wonderful platform, but it's best to know your business reasons for joining before you start posting. Here are some of the top reasons why businesses join Instagram:

>> **Brand awareness:** Make your brand recognized by potential customers.

>> **Engagement:** Meet and interact with your potential customers.

>> **Increase web traffic:** Drive traffic to your website or blog.

>> **Content distribution:** Disseminate useful information about your product.

>> **Lead generation:** Collect data for list building and sales prospecting.

>> **Community building:** Gather a community of people who love and engage with your brand.

>> **Customer support:** Answer questions, field complaints, and accept compliments.

Assembling your Instagram team

You might have only one business reason for using Instagram, or you might have all seven! The number of reasons you choose dictates the roles and responsibilities in managing the account. And your budget plays a big role in determining whether you or a team shoulder those responsibilities. Regardless of the number of people, certain functions must be established for your business to be successful on Instagram.

Social media manager

Generally, the *social media manager* is responsible for the account's big picture. In regards to your business goals, the social media manager plans the strategy of the account and might assist in hiring team members for the other roles (discussed next). The social media manager also creates the account, manages passwords, and sets up the profile page. Details on how to do all these tasks are in Chapters 1 and 2. If you're a one-person team, you'll take on the role of social media manager and all the other roles described in this section.

Content creator

The *content creator* creates and organizes all content to be shared in the account. It's best if the content creator has experience with photography and graphic design because Instagram is visual and success on the platform requires professional imagery. The content creator may also be responsible for posting, scheduling, and storing posts to be shared later. Details about creating a content calendar are detailed later in this chapter.

Community manager

Community managers are in charge of engagement. They should be regularly following other accounts, and liking and commenting on posts from other Instagrammers. A community manager should be actively listening to your audience and those in the your online community so he or she can anticipate problems or take advantage of opportunities to promote the brand. The community manager is the PR arm of your Instagram account.

Campaign manager

Promotions, contests, and giveaways are used to attract more followers. The *campaign manager* manages them all. A promotion might include paid advertising or working with other accounts for shared exposure. The campaign manager works closely with the content creator, often providing a storyboard of ideas.

Analytics manager

The *analytics manager* tracks all data in the account. Followers, post performance, campaign results, hashtag winners, you name it — the analytics manager tracks it. After this data is collected, the analytics manager shares it with the team so they can make informed decisions about what is and isn't working.

Determining your brand voice

Does your brand have a consistent voice? For instance, if someone doesn't see your physical branding (logo, colors, imagery), could he or she recognize that the content was from you simply by the words that were written? Establishing a consistent brand voice is important, especially if you have several content creators.

Here's how to get started:

» **Review several samples of your content and pull the pieces that you feel best represent what you (and your team, if you have one) want to convey as your brand.** Figure out what they all have in common. Also note which items don't fit so you'll know what you don't want your brand voice to sound like.

>> **Choose three words that best describe your brand from the pile of sample content.** For instance, a daycare might choose *nurturing, diverse,* and *joyful.* Then further break down how these words will be expressed by your brand. For example:

- Nurturing: Loving, safe, cuddly, warm, kind, patient

- Diverse: Multiple programs, cultural awareness, inclusive

- Joyful: Happy, fun, musical, laughter

>> **If you have a team, ensure that they are on board with the brand voice and the associated words.** Show them your favorite pieces of content that embody these words so they have a good understanding about how you want them used.

>> **Review your brand voice at least every six months to make sure it's still working.** Look over a large sample of content to see how your brand voice has been carried out, and adjust anything that isn't working. You may even discover a new word that you'd like to incorporate!

Envisioning your look

After you have an understanding of your brand's voice, it's time to work on your brand's look. Although most people consider the logo the main element of a brand, you need to consider a lot more. In the context of Instagram, usually your content, not the logo, is the focal point of your profile. However, your logo makes a good starting point upon which to base other elements.

A logo is a distinctive symbol that the public can easily identify as part of your brand. Think of some of the brands you see regularly, such as Target, Apple, and Starbucks. One look at those logos and you instantly know which company is represented.

Logos can be designed in a variety of ways:

>> As an object that's easily associated with the product or service, such as the smoking wine bottle from Smoking Gun Wines (see Figure 3-1, left).

>> As an abstract symbol that isn't obviously related with the product or service, such as the symbol that Marketing Specialist uses with the company name (see Figure 3-1, center).

>> As a wordmark logo, in which the name of the business is the logo set in a consistent font and color, such as the Jenn's Trends logo (see Figure 3-1, right).

FIGURE 3-1:
These logo types
illustrate an easily
associated
product or
service (left),
an abstract
symbol (center),
and a wordmark
logo (left).

The company's color palette, brand voice, company's values and, of course, brand name should all be integrated with the logo. A professional graphic designer can work with you to select colors, advise on fonts that enhance your brand voice, and assist in drawing or selecting visual objects to represent your brand. A graphic designer is also familiar with the different file types necessary for print versus online and should provide the logo in several formats for different uses. We recommend that you use a professional for this instead of creating a logo on your own.

After your logo is created, you'll likely have one or two colors established with your brand. It's nice to develop a fuller color palette of complementary colors that you can use in your marketing content. Remember to consider your brand voice when selecting these colors. Most colors illicit a mood (for example, blue is calming and red can mean anger), so do some research or have your graphic designer help create a full color palette when he or she develops your logo.

Next, focus on creating a consistent style for your images. Choices for your images can vary by using the following:

» Photography, illustrations, videos, or any combination thereof: In Figure 3-2, left, @kailochic uses photography exclusively as its Instagram style. In Figure 3-2, center, @webvideoads uses video as its style.

» Text overlays on all, some, or no images: In Figure 3-2, right, @mollymarshall marketing uses text overlays on all her images.

» Only certain colors: @laurabriedis.design uses pink, blue, and purple as the dominant colors in all the images chosen for her Instagram style, as you can see in Figure 3-3, left.

» Only certain subject matter: In Figure 3-3, right, @bruce_the_office_cat features one cat hanging around the office as the main subject in all its images.

FIGURE 3-2:
Instagram business accounts often showcase one image style, such as photography (left), videos (middle), or text overlays on images (right).

© Kara Whitten (left), Ahryn Scott (middle), and Molly Marshall Marketing (right)

By setting your business goals, assembling your team (even if that team is just you), determining your brand voice, and envisioning your look, you've provided a good foundation. Now you're ready to start thinking about your posts. Read on to find out how to find post ideas.

FIGURE 3-3:
Instagram business accounts often stick to a color scheme (left), or one subject matter (right).

© Laura Briedis (left), ©Graphics and More (right) — this is where Bruce the cat lives

Gathering Post Ideas

If you've completed the steps outlined earlier in this chapter, you can now get down to the fun part: finding post ideas! Researching your competition, deciding on a post type, and creating a content calendar are covered next to keep you on the path to an awesome Instagram page!

Researching your competition

Chances are you already have a good idea about who your competition is offline, especially if your business serves customers locally. If you have several business names to research, finding them on Instagram is fairly easy if they each have an account.

Here are two easy ways to find the Instagram accounts of your competitors:

>> Go to their websites and see whether they have a link to their Instagram accounts. If so, click the link or Instagram icon.

>> Go to Instagram directly and click the magnifying glass at the bottom of the page to display the Search field. Type the business name in the Search field (see Figure 3-4) and see whether the business appears. Tap the name to go to the account.

TIP

If you're using the second research method, several accounts might have similar names. If you can't distinguish which one is the correct account, use the first method to verify that you've found the correct one.

After you locate a competitor's Instagram account, look at its profile page. Some businesses take more care with their profile page than others. Ask yourself the following:

>> Does it have an easily identifiable username?

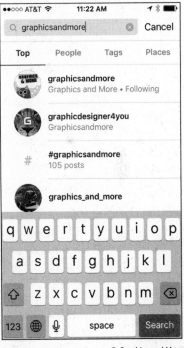

© Graphics and More

FIGURE 3-4:
Type a business name in the Search field, and look for its Instagram account in the list that appears.

>> Is that account set up as a business account? (Call, Email, and Directions buttons are displayed only on business accounts, as shown in Figure 3-5.)

>> Does it explain what the business does in a simple way?

>> Has it included a link to its website or another resource?

>> Are photos, images, and videos used in a cohesive way?

>> Does it have an Instagram story running?

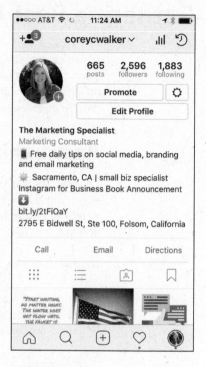

Look at what your competitor has done. Can you learn any lessons, good or bad, for your own profile? For more information about creating a winning profile, see Chapter 2.

Next, tap the last photo that the competitor's account posted. Take note of the image and caption. Does the post

FIGURE 3-5:
A business profile can display buttons for Call, Email, and Directions.

>> Have an intriguing image, video, or photo?

>> Use text overlays that might include a quote, phrase, or statistic?

>> Use filters? If so, is one filter used consistently?

>> Have a caption? If so, does it make you want to know more?

>> Use hashtags? If so, how many?

Go through this set of questions with several of your competitor's posts. Note which of them received the highest engagement, including likes and comments. Also note the posts that received low engagement.

If you'd like to get more technical, set up an Excel spreadsheet using the preceding questions as column headings and note similarities between winning and losing posts. Repeat the process with other competitors. Then use the information to craft posts that are more attractive to your target audience.

TIP

This process doesn't need to be restricted to competitor research alone. Feel free to see what other brands are doing successfully on Instagram and determine whether their techniques can be translated to your business.

Determining post content

If you did the research described in the last section, you'll have a good idea of what content is working (and what's not) for your competitors and other brands. Now that you have the data you need, plus the work you've done on your brand, you're ready to go!

You should now know the following:

>> Your brand voice

>> Your color palette

>> Whether you'll be using photography, illustrations, video, or all three

>> Whether text overlays will be used sometimes, always, or never

>> Whether you'll be using a filter, and which one

>> Your caption style

>> How many hashtags you'll use (for information on hashtag research, head to Chapter 8)

If you're still struggling for content ideas, think about the following quick, effective content ideas for your posts:

>> How-to articles related to your industry (by using a link in the bio)

>> Product or service success stories and testimonials (by using a link in the bio)

>> Case studies (by using a link in the bio)

>> Weekly hashtag themes, such as #TBT (Throwback Thursday) or #WCW (Woman Crush Wednesday)

>> Holidays

>> Behind-the-scenes photos of your staff

TIP

For more post ideas, see Chapter 18.

After you have the type of content for your posts figured out, the next step is creating a content calendar.

Creating a content calendar

A *content calendar* is an excellent way to get your content organized. It forces you to think strategically, which is far better than putting last-minute random content on your profile. It also provides an easy way to share plans with your team and offers a complete snapshot at the end of the year for planning the next year. An Instagram content calendar should

>> Include one to six months of planning.

>> Tie in with your other marketing functions and campaigns.

>> Account for holidays (including wacky ones such as #NationalDonutDay) if you choose to celebrate them.

>> Account for major industry events.

>> Include dates of product or service launches.

>> Include space for regularly scheduled tips, articles, and how-to's.

>> Save space for curated content from others.

>> Set aside dates for tying in Instagram stories and video with your regular Instagram posts.

>> Note whether a post will be a paid ad and how much you'll spend.

If you want to start simply, set up a content calendar in Excel or Google Sheets. Create a worksheet for each month of the year, and then type each day of the week across the top. On the left, separate the rows by weeks, for instance July 2 – July 8, 2018, as shown in Figure 3-6. Add a row below each date if you also plan to do Instagram stories on a regular basis.

	A	B	C	D	E	F	G	H
	Days/Weeks	Monday	Tuesday	Wednesday	Thursday	Friday	Saturday	Sunday
1								
2	July 2 - July 8, 2018 Posts							
3	Stories							
4	July 9 - July 15, 2018 Posts							
5	Stories							
6	July 16 - July 22, 2018 Posts							
7	Stories							
8	July 23 - July 29, 2018 Posts							
9	Stories							
10								

FIGURE 3-6: A simple content calendar set up in Excel.

After you set up the framework, start filling in known items, such as holidays, events, promotions, and contests you've planned. You'll be surprised how quickly your content calendar fills up, but there will still be several empty spaces. These empty spaces are the perfect spot for setting dates for tips, articles, how-to's, infographics, and curated content from others. See Figure 3-7 for an example of a content calendar for an outdoor equipment retailer.

FIGURE 3-7:
This content
calendar shows a
one-month plan
for an outdoor
equipment
retailer.

	A	B	C	D	E	F	G	H
1	Days/Weeks	Monday	Tuesday	Wednesday	Thursday	Friday	Saturday	Sunday
2	July 2 - July 8, 2018 Posts	Campfire smores	4th of July	Best hiking article	Tent sale promo	Mt. Lassen photo	25% off tents today	
3	Stories	Boomerang of campfire	Fireworks	Jax on hike	Walk-through of best tents in store		C'mon down to the sale!	
4	July 9 - July 15, 2018 Posts	Lake Tahoe photo	Mountain biking event photos			20% off hiking equip	Mt. Zion photo	
5	Stories	Boating on Tahoe video	Behind the Scenes of biking event			Pics of hiking shoes on sale		
6	July 16 - July 22, 2018 Posts	#GoCamping promo with user generated photos all week						
7	Stories	Send us your camping photos! Camper takeover!						
8	July 23 - July 29, 2018 Posts	Backpack sale		Fall camping article		#FreeCarabinerDay		Backpack sale
9	Stories	Sarah modeling backpacks		Leaves falling video - get ready for Fall	Carabiners falling from bin video			

If you've been on other social media platforms for a while, you may have tons of this content waiting to be reformatted for Instagram. But if you're new to social media, a brainstorming session is helpful for thinking of creative new posts.

Now that you have a plan, you can move on to creating the content. Chapters 4 and 5 have in-depth information about taking photos and creating videos. If you plan on creating posts with text overlays or other designed images, dozens of apps make it quick and easy for anyone. Here are some to try out:

>> **Adobe Spark** (https://spark.adobe.com/): Social media graphic templates to repurpose, including one for Instagram Stories

>> **Canva** (www.canva.com): Social media graphic templates, photography, fonts, and images available for free or $1

>> **PicLab** (http://museworks.co/piclab/): Features for creating photo collages and specialty sticker overlays

>> **Typic** (www.typicapp.com/): Includes filters, creative text overlays, and stickers

>> **WordSwag** (http://wordswag.co/): Backgrounds and free photography plus several fonts and suggested famous quotes available for text overlays

In the next section, you find out about the best places to store and schedule all of this glorious content.

Evaluating third-party scheduling and analytics platforms

Excel and Google Sheets are excellent tools for planning the timing, topics, and titles of posts, but they're not meant to be used to store images for posting later. Luckily, several platforms allow you to store, schedule, and analyze your Instagram posts. But unlike Facebook or Twitter, Instagram has a tricky little clause in its terms and conditions that doesn't allow you to schedule a post; Instagram prefers that people post in the moment.

Several platforms offer a work-around for this snag — allowing you to upload and store your image and caption in advance without publishing it for you. The steps are similar on all platforms:

1. The platform sends you a push notification on your phone (see Figure 3-8, left) when your scheduled posting time arrives.

2. The platform shows you the image and caption, automatically brings the image into Instagram, and copies the caption text (see Figure 3-8, right).

3. You can select a filter, and then the final share screen appears where you can paste the caption.

4. Tag people or a location, or share to your other networks, and then tap Share.

FIGURE 3-8:
Third-party schedulers such as Hootsuite send a notification to your phone at your scheduled post's time (left) and then allows you to publish the stored image and text (right).

© Graphics and More

These steps aren't as convenient as scheduling for Facebook or Twitter, where you can set it and forget it, but it's what's available for now!

Another function that many third-party platforms offer (and many businesses overlook) is analytics. You can learn quite a bit about your customers' preferences by paying attention to data.

For instance, simply looking at which posts received the highest likes or comments in the last month unveils big clues about what you should post next. You'll probably notice that certain images or background colors work better. Data can also reveal which time of day is best to post, or whether certain hashtags attract more people. For specifics on Instagram analytics, head to Chapter 14.

As of this writing, the most common third-party platforms that enable Instagram post scheduling (with push notifications) and analytics are

» Buffer

» Hootsuite

» Later

» Planoly

» Sprout Social

Other services included on most of the platforms listed follow:

» Connections to other networks, such as Facebook, Twitter, LinkedIn, and Google+

» Engagement (commenting, liking, following) with other accounts

» The capability to share scheduled posts with other members of your team and track approvals

» The capability to manage multiple accounts at once on a dashboard, such as the one in Figure 3-9

Do your homework by looking at the services available and comparing the pricing on each platform. (Pricing structures vary wildly.) Some platforms are robust but may have more than you'll realistically use. Imagine how you would use the platform on a daily basis, look at your budget, and then make your choice.

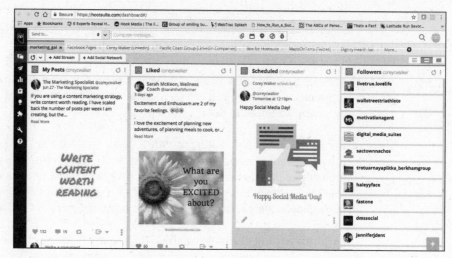

FIGURE 3-9:
Many platforms, such as Hootsuite, offer a dashboard so you can see multiple streams of content in one place.

TIP

If you use multiple social media networks for your business, choose a platform that uses a dashboard, such as Hootsuite or Sprout Social, so you can view all your accounts easily.

2

Creating Your Narrative

IN THIS PART . . .

Take a photo in the Instagram app on your smartphone or tablet.

Share photos from your Camera Roll, Gallery, or computer hard drive.

Record one or more video clips in the Instagram app on your smartphone or tablet.

Add more to the story with photo or video descriptions.

Chapter **4**

Taking and Posting Great Photos

Now that you have all your Instagram ducks in a row, it's time for those ducks to start walking around . . . and take some photos.

In this chapter, you find out how to take photos with Instagram, use editing tools to make your photos look their best, and then share photos stored on your iPhone, iPad, or Android smartphone or tablet with your followers and on other social networks.

REMEMBER You can upload photos only in the Instagram app on your smartphone or tablet.

All figures in this chapter were taken using the iPhone app, because that's Instagram's native platform. Don't worry, Android users — we note any differences between the iPhone and Android apps.

Taking Your Best Shot

Before you can post a photo on Instagram, you need to tell the app where to get the photo. In this section, we cover taking a photo. For details on selecting from your existing photos, see the "Uploading Photos from Your Camera Roll" section, later in the chapter.

When you first log in to Instagram, you'll see your feed on the screen. Tap the + icon at the bottom of the screen. When prompted, allow Instagram access to your phone's camera. Next, you'll see the Photo screen shown in Figure 4-1.

The good news is that you have to go through this process only once. The next time you open Instagram and tap the + icon, you won't have to enable camera access.

Note the following elements in the Photo screen:

>> The *viewer* appears in the top part of the screen.

>> The *switch cameras icon* (two circular arrows) is in the bottom-left corner of the viewer. Tap the icon to switch between your smartphone's front and back cameras.

© Soap & Sprinkles

FIGURE 4-1:
Now you can take your picture.

>> The *flash icon* (lightning bolt in a circle) appears in the bottom-right corner of the viewer. Tap the flash icon to toggle the following flash modes:

- Off: This mode is the default. The icon circle appears hollow.

- On: The circle is white and the lightning bolt appears hollow.

- Auto-detect: The circle is white with an *A* inside.

>> The *shutter button* is the large gray circle in the bottom half of the screen.

>> The *Cancel button,* in the upper-left corner, returns to your Instagram feed.

When you're ready to take a photo, tap the shutter button. Your phone makes a camera shutter sound, as it does when you use the phone's Camera app.

Improving Your Best Shot

The photo you've just taken appears in the viewer of the Filter screen, as shown in Figure 4-2. The screen contains the following four sections, from top to bottom:

>> The *top menu bar*, with a < (back) icon on the left, the Lux icon in the center (which you learn about later in this chapter), and the Next link on the right

>> The *viewer*, which displays your photo

>> A row of *filter thumbnail images* so you can see what your photo will look like with a filter applied

>> The *bottom menu bar*, with a Filter menu option (selected by default) and the Edit option

TIP

Not interested in editing your photo? Simply tap the back icon in the upper-left corner to save your photo and take a new one, if you want.

© Soap & Sprinkles

FIGURE 4-2:
The Filter screen.

Applying a filter

Below your photo in the viewer is a row of filters. Each filter includes a thumbnail image so you can see the filter's effect on your photo.

Swipe from right to left in the row of thumbnail images to view all 23 filters, from Clarendon to Nashville. (Normal is the default image, without a filter.) Tap a filter thumbnail image, and the photo in the viewer changes to show you the photo with that filter applied.

REMEMBER

To return to the original photo, tap the Normal thumbnail (refer to Figure 4-2). To continue processing the photo with a filter, either tap Edit at the bottom-right corner of the screen to edit your photo further, or tap Next in the upper-right corner of the screen to add a description to your photo. (You learn how to add a description in the "Enriching Your Photo" section, later in this chapter.)

What happens when a filter is not quite to your liking and you'd like to tweak it? You can change the intensity of any filter (except Normal) by tapping the filter thumbnail image again. A slider appears; move it to the left and right to change the intensity. The photo in the viewer changes to reflect the selected intensity. The default intensity for each filter is 100. (And yes, we checked each one.) When you've set the intensity to just the right amount, tap Done. If you're still not satisfied and want to return the photo to its original intensity, tap Cancel.

REMEMBER

Keep in mind that any filter settings will revert to the default after you leave this screen.

TIP

If you want to see how the photo with a filter compares to the original photo, tap and hold down on the viewer to view the original photo. Release your finger to see the photo with the applied filter.

Changing the order of filters

Too many filters or your favorite ones are too far down in the list? No problem. Swipe to the end of the filter list, and you'll see a Manage icon. Tap the icon to open the Manage Filters screen, shown in Figure 4-3, where you can perform three tasks: change the order of filters in the row, add filters, and disable filters.

The filters on the Manage Filters screen appear in the same order as they do in the Filter screen. You can change the order of filters as follows:

1. **Tap and hold down on a filter name in the list.**

   The filter name gets larger after you hold down on the name for about a second.

2. **Move the name in the list.**

   As you move the filter name, other filter names helpfully move out of the way so you can see where your selected filter will appear in the list.

3. **When the filter is where you want it, release your finger.**

   The filter name appears in your desired location in the list.

Manage Filters		Done
Clarendon		⊘
Gingham		⊘
Moon		⊘
Lark		⊘
Reyes		⊘
Juno		⊘
Slumber		⊘
Crema		⊘
Ludwig		⊘
Aden		⊘

FIGURE 4-3:
Swipe up and down in the Manage Filters screen to view the entire list of filters.

That's all there is to it! To return to the Filter screen, tap Done.

Adding a filter

When you swipe up and down in the list of filters on the Manage Filters screen, you'll see several filter names that appear dimmed. These filters are disabled, but it's easy to add any of them to the Filter screen.

Simply tap a dimmed filter name. The name turns black, which means the filter is active, and you see a check mark to the right of your newly activated filter name. Tap Done, and you return to the Filter screen, where you see your new filter in the row of filters.

Disabling a filter

If you decide that you don't want to include one or more filters in the Filter screen, you can disable it by tapping the filter name in the list on the Manage Filters screen. The check mark to the right of the name disappears and the filter name is gray. (To add it back, just tap the disabled filter name again.)

When you're finished, tap Done.

Tweaking with the editing tools

When you've finished experimenting with filters, view Instagram's editing tools by tapping Edit at the bottom of the screen. A row of editing tools appears below the viewer, as shown in Figure 4-4.

Swipe from right to left in the row of editing tools to see all 13 tools. Tap a tool to open it below the viewer.

What you see below the viewer depends on the tool you tapped. For example, when you tap the Brightness tool, a slider appears so you can increase or decrease the photo's brightness. No matter what tool you use, the photo in the viewer reflects the changes you make.

Here's what you can do with each tool:

>> **Adjust:** You can adjust your photo in several ways by using the Adjust tool.

© Soap & Sprinkles

FIGURE 4-4:
The tool name appears above each tool icon.

A row of three icons and an associated slider bar appear below the photo, as shown in Figure 4-5, so you can make the following changes:

© Soap & Sprinkles

FIGURE 4-5:
Use the slider bar in the Adjust screen to change the photo's perspective.

- Change the vertical or horizontal perspective of the photo by tapping the left or right icon, respectively, below the photo. After you tap the icon, it's highlighted in black. The slider bar is a series of vertical lines. Swipe left and right in the slider bar to see the change reflected in the photo. As you slide, the highlighted icon above the slider bar is replaced with a box that shows you the change amount measured in degrees.

- If the object in your photo appears tilted, tap the straighten icon in the middle of the icon row. Then swipe left and right in the slider bar to tilt the photo so that the object appears straight. As you swipe in the slider bar, a box appears in place of the straighten icon and shows you the number of degrees you're tilting the photo.

- Rotate the photo 90 degrees counterclockwise by tapping the rotate icon in the upper-right corner of the screen. Keep tapping the rotate icon to continue to rotate the photo in the viewer.

- Crop the photo to a specific area by first zooming in (touch the photo and spread your thumb and index finger apart) in the viewer. Then hold down on the photo and drag it in the viewer until you see the part of the photo you want to post on your Instagram feed. If you decide you don't want to crop the photo, zoom back out to the photo's original size by pinching your thumb and index finger together in the viewer.

>> **Brightness:** In the slider bar below the viewer, slide the dot to the left to darken the photo or to the right to make the photo brighter. As you move the slider bar, the photo in the viewer darkens or brightens accordingly.

>> **Contrast:** In the slider bar, make the light areas of your photo even lighter by sliding the dot to the left. Make the dark areas even darker so the focus is on the lighter areas of your photo by sliding the dot to the right.

TIP

>> **Lux tool:** At the top center of the Filter and Edit screens is an icon that looks like a half-light, half-dark sun. Tap it to open the Lux tool, which you can use to quickly change the exposure level and brightness instead of using the separate Brightness and Contrast editing tools. Move the slider to change the exposure level and brightness. When you're finished, tap Done to save your changes, or tap Cancel to discard them.

If you want to undo any edits you've made, tap the Lux icon and then move the slider to its default location, 50. (The default setting for the Brightness and Contrast editing tools, however, is 0.) When you're done, tap Done. If you've undone any edits in tools other than Lux, you won't see the gray dot below the tool button.

>> **Structure:** This tool enhances the details in the photo, such as adding color in an area that appears washed out in the original. In the slider bar, slide the dot to the right to see how the tool increases the details of the photo in the viewer. If you think the photo is too detailed, slide to the left to make the photo fuzzier.

>> **Warmth:** In the slider bar below the viewer, slide the dot to the right to make the colors warmer by adding orange tones or to the left to make the colors cooler by adding blue tones.

>> **Saturation:** In the slider bar, slide the dot to the right or left to increase or decrease, respectively, the intensity of all colors in your photo.

>> **Color:** You can change the color of your photo's shadows or highlights or both, as well as change the intensity of the tint. Eight colors are available: yellow, orange, red, pink, purple, blue, cyan, or green, as you see in Figure 4-6.

- *To change the color of shadows in your photo:* Tap Shadows, if necessary (it's the default), and then tap one of the color dots.

- *To change the highlight color:* Tap Highlights, and then tap one of the eight color dots, which are the same colors as those used for shadows.

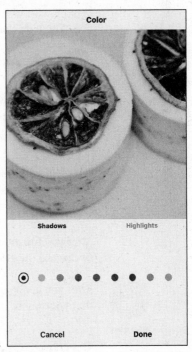

© Soap & Sprinkles

FIGURE 4-6:
Tap the color dot to select a color for your photo shadow.

- *To change the tint intensity for the shadow or highlight color:* Tap the color dot twice. In the slider bar that appears below the viewer, slide the dot to the left or right to decrease or increase the intensity, respectively. When the intensity looks good to you, release your finger from the dot and then tap Done to return to the Color page.

» **Fade:** Do you want your photo to look like it's been sitting in a shoebox for years . . . or decades? In the slider bar, slide the dot to the right to fade the color from your photo or to the left to add color.

» **Highlights:** In the slider bar, slide the dot to the right to increase the brightness in bright areas of the photo. Slide to the left to darken the bright areas in the photo.

» **Shadows:** In the slider bar, slide the dot to the right to lighten the dark areas in your photo. Slide to the left to darken the dark areas.

» **Vignette:** This tool allows you to darken the edges of the photo so people will focus on the center of the photo. In the slider bar, slide the dot to the right to darken the photo edges.

» **Tilt Shift:** You can blur the outer edges of your photo and keep the center in clear focus so people will automatically look at the focused area. Tap Radial below the viewer to blur all four edges of the photo and keep the center focused. Tap Linear to blur just the top and bottom edges of the photo.

You can change the size of the "unblurred" area of the picture by tapping the center of the photo with your thumb and forefinger. Then spread them apart to make the area larger or together to make the area smaller. Tap Off if you don't like the changes and want to keep your entire photo in focus.

» **Sharpen:** This tool sharpens features that aren't visible in the original photo, such as the texture on a wall. In the slider bar, slide the dot to the right and left to make the photo less and more fuzzy, respectively.

After you finish making changes to your photo, apply your effect by tapping Done. Or discard the effect by tapping Cancel.

REMEMBER

After you apply an effect, a gray dot appears below the effect's icon as a reminder that your photo now sports that effect.

Saving your changes (or not)

When you've finished using the editing tools and filters, you can do one of three things:

>> **Discard your changes** and return to the Photo screen by tapping the left arrow icon in the upper-left corner and then tapping Discard in the pop-up menu.

>> **Save your changes and continue editing** by tapping the left arrow icon and then tapping Save Draft in the pop-up menu.

>> **Add a description** to the photo by tapping Next in the upper-right corner. The New Post screen appears, where you can add a caption and location, tag friends, and decide if you want to share the photo on other social networks. (See the next section.)

To follow along with the example in this chapter, tap Next.

Enriching Your Photo

After you tap Next in the Edit screen, the New Post screen appears, as shown in Figure 4-7. (This screen is called Followers on an Android smartphone.) In this screen, you can add a caption to your photo, tag people who appear in the photo, include the photo's location, share the photo on other social media networks, and turn commenting on and off.

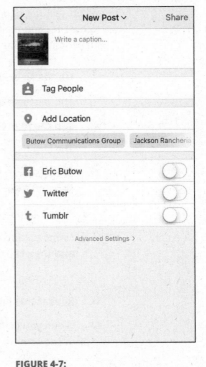

Describing your photo

To add a description to your photo, tap in the top section where it says *Write a caption.* A keyboard appears at the bottom of the screen.

REMEMBER

Captions can't exceed 2,200 characters. You'll know you've reached the limit when you keep typing and no characters appear in the caption box.

FIGURE 4-7:
Add details to your photo here.

TIP

To add a blank line between paragraphs, tap the Return key after the last character of text. If you tap Return after a blank space after the last character, Instagram won't format your paragraph correctly when you post your photo. You can read more about formatting your caption (and the pitfalls) for the iPhone and Android smartphones at www.jennstrends.com/how-to-format-instagram-captions/.

When you've finished writing, tap OK in the upper-right corner of the screen. The text of your caption appears in the caption box.

To edit the caption, tap in the caption box and make your changes. When you're finished, tap OK.

It's good to have options

Below the caption box are five options to identify people in your photo, add a location to your photo, share your photo on other social networks, and turn commenting on and off (under the Advanced Settings link at the bottom).

Tagging people

When you *tag* people, you add their Instagram usernames to your photo so they know that you posted a photo with them in it. Instagram enables you to tag up to 20 people in a single photo. To tag a person in your photo, do the following:

1. **On the New Post (or Followers) screen, tap Tag People.**

   The Tag People screen appears.

2. **Tap the photo to tag.**

   The Search screen appears.

3. **In the Search for a Name box, type the name of the person you want to tag, and then tap the Search key in the keyboard.**

   A list of people appears below the box.

4. **Swipe up and down in the list until you find the person you want to tag, and then tap the person's name.**

   You can tag only people who appear in the list.

5. **Repeat this process to tag more people.**

6. **When you've finished tagging people, tap Done in the upper-right corner of the screen.**

WARNING

Be sure that you tag only people who are in the photo. If you tag someone who isn't in the photo, the tagged person may report you to Instagram, and then you may be subject to "deleted content, disabled accounts, or other restrictions" per Instagram's Community Guidelines. However, if the photo contains a logo or product, you can tag the brand or company associated with the product or logo.

Adding your location

You can include your current location in the photo's description. Tap Add Location. Your smartphone or tablet asks if the Instagram app can use your location if it's the first time you are adding a location. Tap Allow in the pop-up window to continue.

In the Locations screen that appears, swipe up and down in the list of nearby locations. If you don't find your location, tap the Search box at the top of the screen and start typing. As you type, results that most closely match your search term(s) appear in the list. When you find the location in the list, tap the location name.

If you want to delete the location, tap the delete icon (X) to the right of the location. After you delete the location, you see Add Location again on the screen.

REMEMBER

After you allow the Instagram app to use your location, the next time you open the New Post (or Followers) window, you'll see a row of potential locations below Add Location. Swipe up in the row to view more locations. Tap the location name to select it as your location. You can still add a location by tapping Add Location and either selecting a location from the list or by typing the location in the Search box and then selecting the location in the list.

Facebook

Tap the dot to toggle the Facebook switch from left to right to log into Facebook and post your photo to your Facebook newsfeed as well as to Instagram. If this is the first time you're posting to Facebook, you'll be asked to allow Facebook to access your Instagram account.

TIP

If your shared post links to your personal account, the post is shared only with your Facebook friends. When your shared post links to your business account, the post is shared with the people who follow your Facebook business profile.

Twitter

If you want to tweet the same Instagram photo you're preparing, tap the dot to toggle the Twitter switch from left to right to log into your Twitter account. After you log in, you can share your photo and caption in a tweet. Remember that Twitter will cut off any caption that exceeds 280 characters. If this is the first time you are posting to Twitter from Instagram, you will have to allow Twitter access to your account.

Tumblr

You can post your photo to your Tumblr account as well by tapping the Tumblr dot to toggle from left to right. Tumblr opens so you can log into your account, and then you return to Instagram. When you share your photo and related information in Instagram, you'll share it to your Tumblr feed as well.

You have to tap the toggle dot every time you want to share on Facebook, Twitter, and Tumblr.

REMEMBER

Turning commenting on and off

Before you share your photo, you may not want to take the time to read or respond to comments. You can block your followers from leaving comments about your photo. Begin by tapping the Advanced Settings option at the bottom of the New Post screen (refer to Figure 4-7). In the Advanced Settings screen, tap the Turn Off Commenting dot to toggle from left to right. To return to the New Post screen, tap the left arrow in the upper-left corner.

SHARING ON FACEBOOK IS NATURAL

Consider editing your caption before you share a photo or video on Facebook (as well as Twitter and Tumblr, for that matter). When you remove Instagram hashtags and tweak your caption for your Facebook audience, you'll have a much better chance of reaching more people on Facebook. For example, suppose you have a photo you've posted on Instagram and want to post also on Facebook with the #tbt (throwback Thursday) hashtag. Simply remove the Instagram hashtags and then add the #tbt hashtag. Now when you post your Instagram photo on Facebook, people searching for posts with the #tbt hashtag can find your post.

When you share your Instagram photo or video on Facebook, it appears in your Facebook newsfeed. The post includes the caption in your Instagram photo or video, as well as the photo thumbnail or video cover frame. View a photo by tapping it. Play the video by tapping the play icon in the center of the video cover frame.

If you view your photo on the Facebook website on your computer, you can click Instagram above the caption to view the original post on the Instagram website in another browser tab. When you finish viewing the original post and want to get back to using Facebook, close the Instagram tab.

Posting Your Photos: Ta Da!

Your photo or photos are now ready to share with the Instagram world, so all you have to do is tap Share in the upper-right corner of the New Post screen.

After you post a photo, the home screen appears with your photo at the top, as shown in Figure 4-8. If you've posted several photos in one post, you'll be able to swipe in your post to view them all. Slicker than a box of rocks.

TECHNICAL STUFF

Instagram automatically uploads your photo in the best resolution possible. When you take a photo with a smartphone or tablet that runs iOS or Android, resolution isn't an issue. However, if you upload a photo from your Camera Roll (on the iPhone) or Gallery (on an Android smartphone), check your image settings in a photo-editing app such as Image Size (iPhone and iPad) or Photo & Picture Resizer (Android smartphones and tablets). In the app, see that the photo has a width between 320 and 1,080 pixels with an aspect ratio between 1.91:1 and 4:5. For example, if the photo width is 1,080 pixels, the height can be between 566 pixels (1.91:1 ratio) and 1,350 pixels (4:5 ratio). If your photo height is too low or high, Instagram will automatically crop it to fit the aspect ratio. The moral of this story is to check and crop your photos before Instagram does it for you (probably to your annoyance).

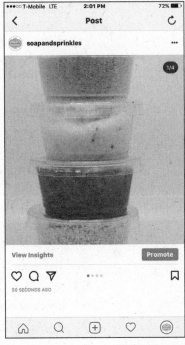

© Soap & Sprinkles

FIGURE 4-8:
The 1/4 in the upper-right of the photo indicates that this post has several photos.

Uploading Photos from Your Camera Roll

Do you have some photos you've already shot that you'd like to share with your followers? It's easy to select one or more photos and then share them on your Instagram feed. Here's how to upload photos from your camera:.

1. **Tap the + icon at the bottom of the home screen.**

   The Photo screen appears.

2. **Tap Library.**

   The Camera Roll screen appears, as shown in Figure 4-9. (Android users see the Gallery screen.) The most recent photo you saved to your smartphone appears in the viewer. Thumbnail-sized photos appear below the viewer.

3. **Swipe in the thumbnail photos to view other photos. When you find one you like, tap it.**

   The selected photo appears in the viewer. Instagram automatically crops your photo to the size of the viewer.

4. **(Optional) View the photo in its original size by tapping the resize icon (labeled in Figure 4-9).**

5. **Tap Next.**

6. **(Optional) Apply filters and edit your photo as described earlier.**

7. **Tap Next.**

   The New Post (or Followers) screen appears.

8. **(Optional) Write a caption, tag people, add a location, change advanced settings and recipients, and share your photo on other social networks.**

   For details, bookmark this page and read the earlier section, "Enriching Your Photo."

9. **When you're ready to share your photos, tap Share.**

© Soap & Sprinkles

FIGURE 4-9:
The thumbnail of the selected photo appears dimmed.

REMEMBER

If you have an Apple Mac desktop or laptop and you use the Safari web browser, there's a trick you can use to upload one or more photos from your Mac to your Instagram profile. Bookmark this page and go back to Chapter 1 to learn all about it. (Windows users, you're out of luck.)

Did you notice in Figure 4-9 the icons for the Boomerang and Layout apps? You use the Boomerang app to create and post mini-videos on your feed. Your camera takes a burst of photos, and Boomerang stitches them together, creating a quick video clip that plays backward and forward — like a Boomerang flies . . . get it? (See Chapter 10 for details on using Boomerang.)

You can use the Layout app to combine multiple photos into one photo and post the combined photo on your feed without having to swipe back and forth between photos.

Uploading Multiple Photos to One Post

You don't need to have one post for each photo. Instead, you can add as many as ten photos in your Camera Roll (or Gallery if you use an Android smartphone) to a single post.

Selecting multiple photos

To choose more than one photo to add to a post, do the following:

1. **In the main Instagram feed screen, tap the + icon.**

2. **Tap Library, in the lower-left corner of the screen.**

   The most recent photo in your Camera Roll (or Gallery) appears in the viewer.

3. **Swipe in the thumbnail photos, and then tap the first photo you want to add.**

4. **Tap the select multiple icon (labeled in Figure 4-9).**

   The selected thumbnail appears dimmed, with a blue number 1, as shown in Figure 4-10.

5. **Tap another thumbnail.**

   The photo appears in the viewer, and a number 2 appears next to the thumbnail. That number shows you the order in which your followers will see the photos in your post.

   REMEMBER

   If you select a photo but then decide that you don't want to include it, just tap the thumbnail photo. The order of your photos will change if you selected more than two photos. To deselect all photos, tap the blue select multiple icon in the lower-right corner of the viewer.

6. **Continue tapping thumbnails as needed.**

   In Figure 4-11, we've chosen three photos. The numbers reflect the order in which we selected each photo.

7. **When you have finished selecting photos, tap Next.**

   The Edit screen appears.

Edit the photos by tapping Next in the upper-right corner of the screen.

FIGURE 4-10:
The select multiple icon in the viewer is blue and the other viewer icons have disappeared.

FIGURE 4-11:
The most recently selected photo appears in the viewer.

TIP

To reorder the photos, you have to deselect them and then reselect them in the correct order. (Yes, this is something Instagram needs to work on.) For example, suppose you select five photos and want to move photos 3 and 4 to positions 4 and 5, respectively. First deselect photos 3 and 4. At this point, the former photo 5 becomes photo 3. Then select the former photo 3, which becomes photo 4, and then select the former photo 4, which becomes photo 5.

Applying filters and adding photos

After you have selected your photos and tapped Next, the Edit screen appears, as shown in Figure 4-12. The top of the screen displays the photo you're editing.

A row of filter types appears below the photo. Swipe from right to left in the row to view all the filters. To apply a filter to all photos in the group, tap the thumbnail image under the filter name.

At the right side of the screen, you see part of the next photo in your photo group. To see the other photos, swipe left. To add another photo to your post, swipe to the end of the row, tap the + icon, and then select the photo from the Camera Roll screen, as described in the "Uploading Photos from Your Camera Roll" section earlier in this chapter.

Editing photos individually

To edit a photo, tap it in the row of photos. The selected photo appears in the center of your screen. Now you can do the following:

>> **Add a filter:** Swipe right to left in the filter row, and then tap the filter thumbnail image. Get all the details in the "Adding a filter" section.

>> **Change the exposure and brightness levels at once:** Tap the Lux icon (half-light, half-dark sun) at the top of the screen. Learn more about using the Lux tool in the "Tweaking with the editing tools" section.

>> **Perform other editing tasks:** Tap Edit, and then follow the instructions in the "Tweaking with the editing tools" section.

Tap Done in the upper-right corner when you're finished.

FIGURE 4-12:
The filter name appears above the filter thumbnail image.

Adding information and sharing your photos

When your photos are the way you want them, tap Next in the upper-right corner of the Edit screen.

In the New Post screen, you can write a caption, tag people, add a location, share your photo on other social networks, and turn commenting on and off as described earlier in the "Enriching Your Photo" section.

TIP

You can't write a caption for each photo when you have multiple photos in your post. So when you write your description, the caption should describe all your photos, not just one.

When you've finished editing your photos, it's time to share them. Tap Share in the upper-right corner of the New Post screen.

Chapter **5**

Recording and Posting Great Videos

I f you've checked your competitors on Instagram and other social-networking websites (you have, haven't you?), you've noticed that they're creating and producing short videos to promote their business. And if they haven't, producing videos of your own is an opportunity to have an advantage over your competition. After all, digital video advertising is expected to grow at double-digit rates every year through 2020 (www.emarketer.com/Article/Digital-Video-Advertising-Grow-Annual-Double-Digit-Rates/1014105).

Instagram added video to its smartphone apps in 2013. Sorry, Windows and Mac users; you can't upload video to Instagram from your computers.

In this chapter, you learn how to record video in the Instagram app by using a smartphone or a tablet. Then you discover how to edit your video with Instagram's built-in editing tools and add a description.

Finally, you find out how to share your video on Instagram and start bringing in viewers and, maybe, customers.

Recording Your Day

Instagram gives you the flexibility to record videos that are as short as 3 seconds or as long as 60 seconds. If you find that 60 seconds is too limiting, use the video as a teaser (think of it as your own movie preview) to get people to click through to your website or to another video website such as YouTube.

Before you record a video, you should know your audience: People younger than 35 prefer 10-second videos, and people 35 and older prefer 30-second spots (www. adweek.com/digital/new-study-shows-millennials-prefer-short-mobile-videos-while-older-crowds-long-form-170739/). Learn more about reaching your audience in Chapter 3.

Filming with a smartphone or tablet

When you're ready to start recording a video on your iPhone, iPad, Android smartphone, or Android tablet, open the Instagram app (if it's not open already) and then tap the + icon at the bottom of the home screen. In the Library or Photo screen that appears, tap Video.

FIGURE 5-1:
If you want to record silent videos, tap Don't Allow.

REMEMBER

The Instagram apps on the iPhone, iPad, Android smartphones, and Android tablets all work the same.

The first time you open the Video screen, a pop-up window appears, as shown in Figure 5-1. Instagram wants to access the microphone on your smartphone so it can record videos with sound. Access the microphone by tapping OK.

REMEMBER

The next time you open the Video screen, you won't see this pop-up window. If you want to turn your microphone off and on in Instagram, access your smartphone's settings, open the Instagram settings entry, and then turn the microphone on or off.

The Video screen has the following elements, all labeled in Figure 5-2:

Return to your Instagram feed

Viewer

Switch cameras

Shutter

FIGURE 5-2:
Tap Cancel if
you decide you
don't want to
record a video.

Minimum 3-second recording time

Recording bar

>> The *viewer*, which is in the upper part of the screen, displays what your smartphone sees through its camera lens.

>> The *switch cameras icon* is in the lower-left corner of the viewer. Tap this icon to switch between the front and back cameras.

>> The *recording bar* is one of two bars just below the viewer and on the left. The recording bar represents how long you've been recording. When the recording bar is blinking, you can start recording either at the beginning of a video or after a video clip. (You find out about recording multiple video clips in the next section.)

>> The *3-second recording time bar* indicates when the video is 3 seconds long. When the recording bar passes the 3-second spot, you can save your video.

>> The *record button* is the large gray circle in the bottom half of the screen.

Start recording by tapping and holding down on the record button. The recording bar expands as you record. (If you reach the 60-second limit, the bar spans the width of the screen and Instagram stops recording.) The amount of time you've been recording appears above the record button, as shown in Figure 5-3. When you've finished recording, release your finger from the record button.

REMEMBER

If you record for only one or two seconds, the recording bar is solid for the time you recorded. Between the recording bar and the minimum bar, you'll see a blinking recording bar. That blinking bar tells you how many more seconds you have to meet the minimum recording time to save your video.

Recording multiple video clips

To save time, you can record multiple clips in one recording. For example, suppose you're recording a video of your new restaurant. After filming the inside of the restaurant, you don't want to spend precious video time recording your move to the outside to show the exterior of the building.

After you record your first clip, release your finger. When you're ready to start recording again, tap and hold down on the record button again. You may repeat this process as many times as you want within the 60-second limit for a video. The timer above the record button continues from the time you paused the recording.

The recording bar places a white line between each clip. In this way, you can see how many clips you have. Figure 5-3, for example, has three clips of varying times.

Deleting video clips

If you decide that you want to delete the last video clip you recorded, tap Delete at the bottom of the screen (refer to Figure 5-2). The color of the Delete button and

FIGURE 5-3:
The black recording bar appears directly below the viewer.

the recording bar changes to red. Then tap Delete again. The Delete option disappears and the blinking recording bar appears so you can record a new video clip.

If you want to delete more clips, just repeat this process. Easy like Sunday morning.

Checking out your video

After you record your video, you'll want to review it before posting. From the Video screen, tap Next. You see the Filter screen, which you learn about in the next section.

WARNING

If you haven't recorded for the minimum 3 seconds, you'll see a pop-up above the minimum bar when you tap Next. This pop-up points to the minimum bar and tells you to record at least to that point. After a few seconds, the pop-up disappears and you can record another clip.

The video starts playing in the viewer. To stop playing the video, tap anywhere in the viewer. To resume, tap the play button, in the middle of the viewer, as shown in Figure 5-4.

TIP

You can toggle video sound on or off by tapping the speaker icon at the top of the page. If you've stopped your video, the video will start playing after you turn the video sound on or off.

FIGURE 5-4:
Begin playing the video by tapping the play icon.

Improving Your Video

You can improve your video in several ways: add a filter, change the cover frame, and trim the video. In this section, you start by applying a filter to your video in the Filter screen.

Applying a filter

Below the viewer is a row of filters. (The Normal, Clarendon, and Amaro filters are shown in Figure 5-4.) The thumbnail image below each filter shows you the filter's effect on your video.

Swipe in the row of thumbnails to view all 23 filters. (Normal is the default, so it isn't considered a filter.) Tap a filter's thumbnail, and the video with the applied filter plays in the viewer.

You can change the intensity of any filter by tapping the filter's thumbnail, and then moving the slider to the left and right. (The default intensity is 100.) As you move the slider, the video reflects the change. When you've finished selecting an intensity, tap Done.

The video continues to play when you apply a new filter or change the intensity of a filter. If you want to return the video to its original state, tap the Normal thumbnail.

Changing the cover frame

Instagram uses the first frame from your video to produce a *cover frame*, which is the frame that appears at the start of your video. You can change the cover frame as follows:

1. **In the Filter screen, tap Cover.**

   The default cover frame appears in the viewer and also below the viewer in a white focus box. The other frames appear next to the focus box and are dimmed, as shown in Figure 5-5.

2. **Tap and hold down on the frame in the focus box, and then drag the frame within the row.**

   As you drag, the focus box moves to another frame in your video and you see this new cover frame in the viewer.

3. **When you find a cover frame you like, release your finger.**

4. **Tap Next.**

FIGURE 5-5:
Frames that aren't selected appear dimmed.

TIP

The cover frame will appear in your Instagram feed, so be sure that the frame you select isn't blurry. You want to make a good impression on your followers as well as your potential customers.

Adding details

In the screen that displays your video (refer to Figure 5-4), tap Next. The New Post screen appears, as shown in Figure 5-6.

In this screen, you can add a caption, include a location where the video was recorded, share the video on other social media networks, and turn commenting on and off. The process for adding all this good stuff is described in Chapter 4. (Note, however, that you can't tag people in videos, so you can skip the instructions about tagging in Chapter 4.)

FIGURE 5-6:
Your video frame appears as a thumbnail in the upper-right corner.

Posting Your Video

When you're ready to post your video, tap Share in the upper-right corner of the New Post screen. After a few seconds, your video appears on the Instagram home screen, as shown in Figure 5-7.

The video starts playing as soon as you view it and will play continuously every time you view the post. The video plays without sound, but you can turn on the sound by tapping the video icon in the lower-left corner of the video. Cool beans.

FIGURE 5-7:
The video plays on the home screen.

Uploading a Stored Video

It's easy to upload a video that you've already recorded and stored on your iPhone, iPad, or Android smartphone or tablet. Simply follow these steps:

1. **Tap the + icon at the bottom of the Instagram feed screen.**

2. **If the Library screen is not displayed, tap Library.**

3. **Select the video you want to upload by tapping its thumbnail image in the Camera Roll or Gallery screen, as shown in Figure 5-8.**

   The video plays continuously in the viewer. Stop playback by tapping anywhere in the viewer.

   Instagram automatically crops your video to the size of the viewer, but you can resize the video to its original size by tapping the resize icon (labeled in Figure 5-8).

4. **(Optional) Apply a filter, change the cover frame, and trim your video.**

   These tasks are described in the "Improving Your Video" section.

5. **Tap Next.**

6. **(Optional) Add a caption and a location, specify other social networks where you want to share your video, and turn commenting on or off.**

   These tasks are the same for photos and videos. For details, see the section on enriching photos in Chapter 4.

TIP

Select up to 10 videos to share in one post

Video run time

FIGURE 5-8:
The selected video thumbnail image is faded so you know it's the video playing in the viewer.

Uploading Multiple Videos from an iPhone or iPad

If you've already taken videos with your iPhone or iPad and saved them to your Camera Roll, you can upload them to a single Instagram video and share it with your followers. Sorry, Android users; this feature isn't available on Android smartphones yet.

Follow these steps to upload multiple clips into one Instagram video:

1. **Tap the + icon in the Instagram feed screen.**

2. **If the Library screen isn't displayed, tap Library.**

3. **Select the first video you want to upload by tapping its thumbnail image in the Camera Roll screen. Then tap Next.**

   The Filter screen appears.

4. **Tap Trim, at the bottom of the screen.**

   The Trim screen appears, and your selected video plays in the viewer, as shown in Figure 5-9.

5. **Tap the + icon, and then tap the thumbnail for the video that you want to add to the first video.**

   The selected video now sports a 2, which tells you that this is the second clip that will appear in the video. This second clip plays continuously in the viewer; to stop playing, tap anywhere in the viewer.

6. **Repeat Step 5 until you've added all the video clips you want.**

   As you add each clip, Instagram assigns it a number indicating its order in the video.

7. **Tap Done.**

   The Trim screen appears, with thumbnails of your video clip in the order in which they will appear in the video. You can add more clips at this point, if you want. (Tap the + icon, tap the clip's thumbnail, and then tap Done.)

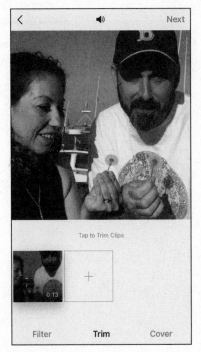

FIGURE 5-9:
The + icon appears to the right of the video thumbnail image.

The viewer displays all the clips playing continuously so you can see how they will appear to your followers. To stop video playback, tap anywhere in the viewer.

WARNING

If you add a clip that puts your video over the 60-second limit, Instagram will automatically trim the last clip so that your entire video lasts for exactly 60 seconds.

8. **(Optional) To remove a clip from your video:**

   a. *Tap and hold down on the clip's thumbnail.* The viewer is replaced by an X inside a box.

   b. *Drag the thumbnail to the X.*

9. **(Optional) Apply a filter or change the cover or both.**

   These tasks are described in the "Improving Your Video" section, earlier in the chapter.

10. **Tap Next.**

    The New Post (Followers) screen appears.

11. **(Optional) Type a caption, add a location, share your photo on other social networks, and turn commenting on or off.**

    For more information, read the section on enriching photos in Chapter 4. All the information there applies also not only to photos but also to videos, with the exception of tagging people. (You can't tag people in a video.)

REMEMBER

When you upload a video with multiple clips, you can't change the orientation of the clips to landscape or portrait. Each clip appears in its original orientation, so keep that in mind when you want to create a video with multiple clips.

3
Planting Your Garden

Chapter **6**

Commenting and Direct Messaging

This chapter tells you all about sharing your Instagram photos and videos. What's more, you'll find out how to encourage people to comment on your posts and how to send a direct message to a commenter.

You start by thinking about what you should and shouldn't share. Next, you discover how to use a link to invite other Instagram users to comment on your posts as well as how to send a direct message to other users. And if you conclude that a comment is inappropriate, you can use Instagram's built-in reporting tool to send feedback and information to the Instagram staff so they can investigate.

Before You Share, Stop and Think

Instagram provides guidelines that protect and nurture not only the larger Instagram community but also you and your business. Every social network, Instagram included, presumes that when you use its service you agree to its terms of use and any other guidelines that social network may set.

As with any social network, you need to be careful about what you post on Instagram because — as you've probably heard many times before — what's posted on the Internet stays on the Internet . . . forever.

When you share photos and videos on Instagram, you strive to promote your business in the best possible light. However, you must also abide by Instagram's Community Guidelines.

If you run afoul of the Community Guidelines, you may be reported to Instagram. The company works hard to make sure that its users are posting photos and videos that meet its standards. If yours don't, Instagram might delete your post, disable your account, or put in place what it ominously calls "other restrictions."

REMEMBER

To read the latest version of the guidelines, visit the Community Guidelines page at `https://help.instagram.com/477434105621119/`.

Following are the most important points in the Community Guidelines:

>> **Share only photos and videos that you've taken.** If you're using someone else's photo or video, be sure to get permission in writing, either online (such as in an email message) or on paper (such as in an Adobe Acrobat document.)

>> **Don't use services that allow you to buy followers or run automated tasks to collect likes, followers, or shares.** Instagram considers such tactics marketing spam and will shut down accounts to curb the problem.

>> **Post photos and videos that are appropriate for a general audience.** Instagram doesn't allow nudity except in specific cases. In addition, don't post graphic photos or videos.

>> **Follow the law.** This point should be self-evident. If it isn't, perhaps you should follow Obi-Wan Kenobi's advice and go home to rethink your life.

Sharing on Other Social Media Sites

It's easy to share photos and videos on Instagram as well as from Instagram to Facebook, Twitter, and Tumblr. We describe how do those tasks in Chapter 4.

Of course, many other social-networking sites are available. In this section, you learn how to create a link that you can embed into other social network posts or email messages.

Copying and pasting a link to another social network

Instagram's capability to share directly with other social networks is limited to Facebook, Twitter, and Tumblr. But other networks, especially business networks such as LinkedIn, are also worthy of your Instagram posts.

Fortunately, Instagram makes it easy for you to get a web address (URL) link to your post that you can copy and paste to other social networks. Here's how:

1. **On the Instagram home screen, tap your profile icon, in the lower-right corner.**

   The Profile screen appears.

2. **Swipe up and down in your Profile screen, if necessary, to find the posted photo or video you want to link to.**

3. **Tap the photo thumbnail or video frame.**

   The Post screen appears. If you tapped a video frame, the video plays in the Post screen automatically.

4. **Tap the menu icon (three dots), which appears at the top right.**

   The menu shown in Figure 6-1 appears.

5. **Tap Share (iPhone or iPad users) or Copy Share URL (Android users).**

   The Share Post (iPhone or iPad) or Share (Android) screen appears.

6. **iPhone and iPad users, tap Copy Link.**

   A message appears for a few seconds, telling you that the link has been copied to the clipboard. Now you can paste the link into a post on another social-networking website or in an email message, as shown in the next section.

To view the post before you send it, click or tap the photo or video. On a smartphone or tablet, you see the original Instagram post. On a computer, you see the post on the Instagram website in a separate browser tab.

Embedding your photo or video on a web page

If you want to share photos or videos on a web page or in a blog post, you can embed them from the Instagram website on your computer.

When you embed a photo or video, you can click or tap the photo or video to open the original post in the Instagram app on your smartphone or tablet.

If you're using a web browser on your computer, the original Instagram post will appear in a separate browser tab. (You may need to log into Instagram to view the post.) When you finish viewing the original post, close the tab to return to the web page you were viewing.

To embed a photo or video, do the following:

1. **On your computer, log into the Instagram website if you haven't done so already.**

2. **Click the profile icon (silhouette of a person), in the upper-right corner.**

   The Profile screen appears.

3. **Click the photo or video you want to share.**

   The screen displays your photo or video and caption, as well as any comments and likes.

4. **Click the menu icon (three dots), at the bottom right of the image, and then click Embed (see Figure 6-2).**

   If you decide that you don't want to embed your code, close the window by clicking anywhere outside the pop-up window or by pressing the Esc key.

5. If you don't want a caption included with the photo or video, deselect (clear) the Include Caption check box.

6. Click the Copy Embed Code button.

FIGURE 6-2:
You can embed your photo or video here.

Now you can use your favorite website design program to paste the embedded code in a blog post or on a web page.

REMEMBER

When you embed one of your Instagram photos or videos on a website or in a blog post, anyone who has access to that website or blog post will be able to see your photo or video.

Sending Photos and Videos Privately

You're not restricted to posting photos and videos to your profile. You can use the Instagram Direct service to send a private message to a single follower or a group of 2 to 15 followers.

You can send the following items in an Instagram Direct message:

» Photos or videos taken with your smartphone or tablet camera

» Photos or videos uploaded to your smartphone or tablet

» A plain old text message

» A hashtag, which your recipient can tap or click to view posts that contain that hashtag

» A location, which your recipient can tap or click to see posts that include that location

Excited? Even a little? In this section, you discover how to send an Instagram direct message on the iPhone and iPad, on your Android smartphone or tablet, or in the Windows app.

Replying to a direct message by sending a photo

If you're already having a private message conversation in Instagram Direct, you can respond by sending a photo (sorry, no videos) to one or more of your followers. Here's how:

1. **Tap or click the Instagram Direct icon, which appears in the upper-right corner (and is shown in the margin).**

   The Direct screen appears, as shown in Figure 6-3. The most recent direct message conversations appear in the list, with the most recent conversation at the top.

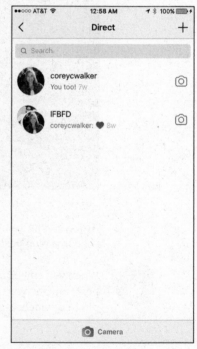

FIGURE 6-3:
Responding to a private message in Instagram Direct.

2. **Tap or click the camera icon to the right of the user name in the list.**

The Camera screen appears with the front camera active. In the Windows app, your webcam becomes active so you can take a photo of yourself. You may be prompted to enable access to your camera or microphone or both.

3. **Take a photo by tapping or clicking the white shutter button at the bottom of the screen or window.**

You can switch between the front and back camera on your iPhone, iPad, Android smartphone, or Android tablet by tapping the switch icon (shown in the margin).

4. **Tap Send.**

Starting a new conversation by sending a photo

When you want to start a new conversation, you don't have to type a message. Instead, you can take a photo and send it to the other person. You can even type a brief caption that will appear on top of your photo.

1. **In the Direct screen, tap or click Camera.**

If you need to get to the Direct screen, first tap or click the Direct icon from the Instagram home screen or window.

2. **Take a photo by tapping or clicking the white shutter button.**

The switch cameras icon appears to the right of the white button so you can switch between the front and rear cameras, if necessary.

3. **If you want to add text in front of your photo, tap or click the text (Aa) icon. Type your message, and then tap Done.**

4. **Tap or click Next.**

The Send To screen appears, as shown in Figure 6-4.

5. **Select your recipients by swiping in the recipient list and then tapping or clicking one or more usernames.**

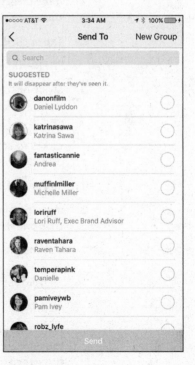

FIGURE 6-4:
Select the recipients here.

After you tap or click a username, a blue circle with a check mark appears to the right and the username appears in the To box above the list.

TIP

You can search for a recipient by tapping the Search box above the list and typing your search terms. As you type, the usernames that most closely match your terms appear in the results list. When you find the name of the recipients you're looking for, tap or click their names in the list.

6. **Tap or click Send.**

   The Direct screen appears and contains the message you sent to the recipient at the top of the conversation list.

Starting a new text conversation and adding a photo

If you prefer to start your conversation with a text message but also want to take a photo or upload a photo or video from your Camera Roll or Gallery, Instagram makes it easy for you to do that, too. Follow these steps:

1. **If the Direct screen isn't open, tap or click the Instagram Direct icon in the upper-right corner.**

2. **Tap or click the add (+) icon.**

   The New Message screen appears.

3. **Swipe or scroll in the list to find the recipients, and then tap or click their usernames.**

   A blue check mark appears to the right of each recipient name after you tap or click it. You can also search for one or more recipients as described in the preceding section.

4. **Tap or click Next.**

5. **If you're an iPhone, an iPad, or a Windows user and have selected more than one recipient, do the following:**

   - *If you want to name this group (so you can send future private messages to all followers in the group), tap the Name This Group box to open the keyboard. Type your name, and then tap the keyboard's Done key.*

   - *If you don't want to name the group, tap or click the X.*

6. **If you want to take a photo on your camera (or webcam if you're using the Windows app), tap or click the camera icon in the lower-left corner of the screen (or window).**

   Follow the instructions for taking a photo in the preceding section.

7. **iPhone, iPad, or Android users: If you want to upload a photo or video from your Camera Roll or Gallery:**

   a. *Tap the mountain range icon.* The Camera Roll or Gallery window appears.

   b. *Swipe in the Camera Roll or Gallery and then tap the thumbnail of the photo or video you want to add.* Your selected photo or video appears in the window. If you selected a video, the video plays continuously.

   c. *Upload the photo or video to your message by tapping the blue up arrow at the bottom of the screen.*

   If you change your mind, close the window by tapping the back icon (<).

8. **To write a message, tap the Write a Message box, type your message, and then tap Send.**

   Your message appears in the Message screen.

9. **Return to the Direct screen by tapping or clicking the < icon.**

   The message you just sent appears at the top of the list. Each message entry in the list shows you the recipients or group name, followed by a brief summary of the last message in the conversation and how long ago the last response was sent.

   View your message on the screen by tapping the message entry. You can also send a follow-up photo to the recipient by tapping the camera icon to the right of the message or group recipient's name and then taking a photo in the camera viewer screen.

10. **Return to the Instagram home screen by tapping or clicking the < icon.**

WARNING

Direct messages are private, and Instagram means it — you can't do several things with a direct message that you can do with a public message:

» You can't share photos or videos sent with Instagram Direct to other social networking websites.

» Any hashtags or locations you add to your private message aren't searchable in Instagram.

» Your messages won't appear in the feed screen or in your profile.

Resuming a previous conversation

If you've had a previous conversation with one or more recipients, you can tap the individual or group name in the Direct screen to view your past conversation(s) and write a new message to start a new conversation. The Message screen appears and you see all the text, photos, and videos you sent previously to that recipient or that group.

Swipe or scroll to view your entire conversation. You can also type a new message, as described previously.

Garnering Comments

After you post a photo or video, any of your followers can comment on it. In this section, we describe two tried-and-true methods to encourage your followers to respond: Include a caption and mention your followers.

Including a caption

A caption adds context to your video and lets people know what they're seeing. If you don't add a caption, your viewers might be confused, and that reflects badly on your business. For example, if you show a photo of your new product but you don't tell viewers what it is and why it's helpful, they may think you don't know what you're doing and you'll be left wondering why you're not getting any attention.

After you create a post and edit your photo or video, you add the caption in the New Post (iPhone or iPad) or Followers (Android) screen.

Do you need more details? Bookmark this page and flip to the section on enriching photos in Chapter 4. The information about adding captions to photos applies also to videos.

Instagram truncates all captions after about three lines of text. If there's more text to read, a More link appears at the end of the truncated text. To read the entire caption, you have to tap or click the link.

TIP

How much text should be in your caption? It's generally a good idea to communicate too much rather than too little, so consider writing one to three short paragraphs. Make sure that the first few lines are enticing enough that your viewer will want to tap or click the More link and read your entire caption.

Mentioning your followers

When one of your followers posts a photo or video, you can leave a like by tapping or clicking the heart icon to the right of the photo or video. To really get a follower's attention, however, you need to write a comment that includes the person's username preceded by the @ symbol. For example, you might type this:

I really like your new business cards, @sideshowbob!

After you mention someone in a comment, that person will receive a notification in his or her feed. And perhaps the person you complimented will be more interested in both finding your latest posts and commenting on them. That, in turn, increases your profile's visibility to other Instagram users when they search for new and interesting profiles.

Reviewing Your Comments

When you get a comment or a like, a notification appears in your feed. You can see how many comments and likes you have for a post by tapping the profile icon in the lower-right corner of the Instagram home screen, swiping until you see the thumbnail of the photo or video you posted, and then tapping the image.

Now you see

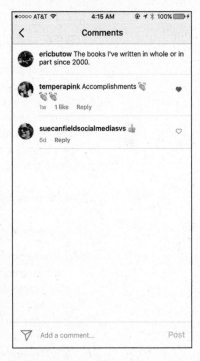

>> The Photo screen if your post contains only one photo

>> The Post screen if your post contains more than one photo

>> The Video screen if your post contains a video

Likes and comments appear below the photo or video. Tap one of the comments or tap the comment icon (cartoon bubble) below the photo or video to open the Comments screen shown in Figure 6-5.

If you want to like the comment without replying to it, tap the like icon (white heart) to the right of the comment. After you tap the icon, the heart turns red and one more like appears for the comment. Return to the Photo, Post, or Video screen by tapping the back icon (<) in the upper-left corner.

FIGURE 6-5:
Your caption appears at the top of the Comments.

If you want to view all your notifications, tap the heart icon at the bottom of the Post, Photo, or Video screen. Then tap the You tab at the top of the Notifications screen if the tab isn't already active. You'll see as many as 100 of your most recent notifications as you swipe in the list. You can view a user's profile by tapping the username in a notification (the username is in bold).

Deciding to respond or delete

You can reply to a comment in two ways, depending on whether you're using the iPhone or iPad, an Android smartphone or tablet, or a computer running Windows.

You can't delete or respond to comments on the Instagram website, though you can add another comment preceded by *@name*, where *name* is the username of the person you're replying to.

iPhone, iPad, and Windows users

If you're using an iPhone, an iPad, or a Windows PC, you can reply to a comment by tapping (or clicking) Reply below the comment.

A second way to reply is to use the comment options. iPhone and iPad users tap and hold down on the comment and then swipe left to display the options shown in Figure 6-6. Windows users should click and hold down on the comment and then move the mouse pointer to the left.

There are three options, from left to right:

>> **Left arrow:** Reply to the commenter.

>> **Exclamation mark:** Report the commenter to Instagram. (You find out more about reporting commenters later in this chapter.) If you delete your own comment, the exclamation mark doesn't appear in the menu. You can report only one commenter at a time.

>> **Trash can:** Delete the comment.

FIGURE 6-6:
The comment options push the comment to the left.

After you delete a comment, a red bar appears at the top of the Comments screen so you can undo the deletion. If you don't tap the bar within five seconds, the comment is deleted permanently.

If you want to close the comment menu without making any changes, tap and hold down on the comment to the left of the menu and swipe to the right. Windows users should click and hold down on the comment and then move the pointer to the right.

When you reply to the commenter using either method (tapping Reply or tapping the left arrow in the comment options), a comment area appears, with the username of the commenter entered automatically. Now you can type your reply and then tap (or click) Post to the right of the comment area.

Have you changed your mind about writing a reply? Tap (or click) the back icon (<) in the upper-left corner of the screen and you'll return to the Photo screen.

Android smartphone and tablet users

Android smartphone and tablet users can reply to a comment by tapping Reply below the comment. The comment area appears with the commenter's username entered automatically. After you type your comment, tap the blue check mark button to the right of the comment area or tap the Send key on the keyboard.

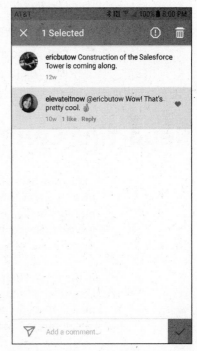

If you want to one or more comments — either your comments or someone else's comments — tap the comment(s). A blue menu bar appears at the top of the screen (see Figure 6-7) that contains the following icons you can tap:

>> **X:** Close the menu bar without making any changes.

>> **Exclamation point:** Report the commenter. (You learn more about reporting commenters later in this chapter.) If you tap more than one comment or you delete your own comment, the exclamation mark doesn't appear in the menu. You can report only one commenter at a time.

FIGURE 6-7:
The number of selected comments appears in the blue bar.

>> **Trash can:** Delete the comment(s).

WARNING

After you delete a comment, a red bar appears at the top of the Comments screen so you can undo the deletion. If you don't tap the bar within five seconds, the comment is deleted permanently.

You can close the menu bar by tapping all the selected comments to deselect them.

Mac and website users

Mac users can use only the Instagram website. If you're using a Mac, another computer, or another device to access the website, you can delete only comments written by someone else — not your own comments.

Here's how to delete a comment:

1. **Click or tap on the profile icon in the upper-right corner of the web page.**

2. **Scroll or swipe until you see the thumbnail of the photo or video that contains the comments.**

3. **Click or tap the thumbnail.**

   The list of comments appears.

4. **Click or tap the X to the right of the comment, and then tap Delete Comment.**

   The comment disappears from the list.

Reporting Commenters When All Else Fails

Instagram asks that you resolve disputes between you and another person who posts a photo, video, or comment that you think may violate Instagram's Community Guidelines. For example, if someone's comment contains inaccurate information about you, you can post a comment or send a private Instagram Direct message and ask the commenter to remove the comment.

If the commenter won't cooperate or the comment is clearly a violation of the Community Guidelines (such as a threat of violence), Instagram strongly recommends that you don't escalate the situation yourself. Instead, report the user to Instagram and have Instagram staffers review the situation.

WARNING

If you refuse to heed Instagram's warning and decide to attack the commenter with nasty comments of your own, you may find yourself in trouble if the commenter reports you for harassment.

Reporting a commenter

Before you report a commenter, review the latest Community Guidelines at `https://help.instagram.com/477434105621119/?helpref=hc_fnav`. If you still believe the commenter must be reported to Instagram for further action, you can use Instagram's built-in reporting tools.

REMEMBER

You can report a user only from your iPhone, iPad, Android smartphone or tablet, or the Windows app. You can't report a user from the Instagram website.

Reporting from an iPhone, an iPad, or the Windows app

If you're reading comments on your iPhone, iPad, or in the Windows app and you come across a comment that violates the Community Guidelines, tap (or click) and hold down on the comment in the list and then swipe (or drag) to the left.

The gray report button appears to the right of the comment. Tap (or click) the button to open the menu at the bottom of the screen, and then select the Spam or Scam option or the Abusive Content option.

If you select Spam or Scam, the menu closes and the comment disappears from the Comments screen so you can continue to read comments. When you tap (or click) Abusive Content, the Report Comment screen opens. You can decide how to report the comment and take any additional steps or get more information. For example, if you choose I Don't Like the Comment, the Blocking People page appears so you can learn how to block commenters.

Reporting from an Android smartphone or tablet

When you see a comment on your Android smartphone or tablet that you think violates the Community Guidelines, tap and hold down on the comment in the list.

The comment gets a light blue background, and a blue bar at the top of the screen tells you that the comment is selected. Tap the exclamation point to open the menu, and then tap one of the reporting options: Spam or Scam, or Abusive Content.

When you tap Spam or Scam, the menu closes and the comment disappears. Now you can get back to reading other comments. When you tap Abusive Content, the Report Comment screen opens so you can decide how to report the comment and take any additional steps or get more information. For example, if you tap This Comment Shouldn't Be on Instagram, you see a list of reasons that you can choose from, such as nudity or pornography.

Blocking a commenter

If a commenter is obnoxious, that alone isn't a reason to report the commenter to Instagram but you can block the commenter. Then you no longer have to read anything from that user again. As on other networking sites such as Facebook and LinkedIn, Instagram doesn't tell users that they've been blocked.

REMEMBER

You can block a user only in the Instagram app on your smartphone or tablet. You can't block a user on the Instagram website.

Here's how to block a user:

1. **In the comments below the photo or from the Comments screen, tap the username of the commenter.**

   The username is the first text you see in the comment and is in bold text.

2. **In the commenter's profile page, tap the three dots in the upper-right corner of the screen.**

   The menu shown in Figure 6-8 appears.

3. **Tap Block.**

Tap or click the < icon to return to the Comments screen. The blocked user's comments no longer appear on the screen. To unblock someone, follow the same steps, except tap Unblock in Step 3.

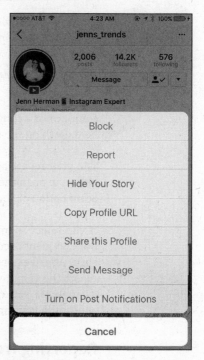

FIGURE 6-8:
Use this menu to block someone from commenting.

Chapter **7**

Finding People to Follow

G rowing your Instagram following is one of the hottest topics on Instagram. If you've spent any time there, surely you've encountered sales pitches to buy followers or purchase a crazy software program to increase likes and follows. Don't do it. Yes, it looks good having a big following, especially when starting out. However, any followers you buy are likely fake accounts, or people who would never buy from you.

In this chapter, you discover how to find followers the right way. First, you follow your Facebook friends who have Instagram accounts, and then you learn how Instagram can access the contact list on your phone to find more followers. Next, you discover ways to explore and search for followers in the Instagram app. Then you look to your competitors' and industry colleagues' follower lists for more ideas. You also learn how to develop an Insta-tribe — an online family that helps and supports you along the way. Finally, after you start getting followers, find out who is worth following back and when it's best not to bother.

Where Are My Peeps?

If you're new to Instagram, you may be wondering where to start. Instagram (and its daddy, Facebook) is happy to help you make connections. You can find people in a few different ways, as you discover in this section.

Finding your Facebook friends

Facebook has a vested interest in making Instagram grow, so it tries to encourage you to round up your Facebook friends and bring them over to Instagram. It's an easy way for you to find people.

To find friends on Facebook, follow these steps:

1. **Go to your Instagram profile page by tapping your photo at the bottom right of your phone's screen.**

2. **Tap the person with a plus (and possibly a red number) at the top left.**

3. **Tap the Facebook link at the top of your screen.**

4. **Confirm your Facebook login by tapping OK.**

   The screen displays how many Facebook friends you have on Instagram (see Figure 7-1).

5. **Tap either Follow All or Follow.**

   To follow every one of your Facebook friends on Instagram, tap Follow All. If you'd rather be more selective, especially because you'll likely be promoting your product or service, you may want to follow friends one by one. Simply tap Follow next to each friend you'd like to connect with, and keep scrolling and following!

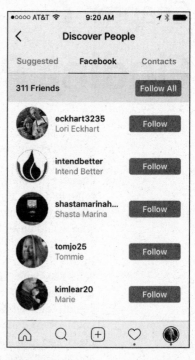

FIGURE 7-1:
Instagram displays all Facebook friends who are available to follow on Instagram.

TIP

Some of your friends may have set their accounts to private. In this case, you see Requested after you tap Follow. They need to approve you before you can view their profile and posts.

Syncing your contact list

Instagram can also connect you with the contacts stored on your phone or tablet. After you activate this feature, your contacts are periodically synced with Instagram's servers. Instagram does not follow anyone on your behalf, and you can disconnect your contacts at any time so that Instagram cannot access them.

WARNING

This feature may be best as a one-and-done in the beginning versus a constant connection for privacy purposes.

To connect your contacts, follow these steps:

1. **Go to your Instagram profile page by tapping your photo at the bottom right of your phone's screen.**

2. **Tap the small person with a plus (and possibly a red number) at the top left.**

3. **Tap the Contacts link.**

   The next screen tells you that Instagram will find people you know, and you're given the option to follow them.

4. **To proceed, tap Connect Contacts.**

   Another pop-up asks whether Instagram can access your contacts.

5. **Tap Allow Access.**

   A pop-up appears asking you to allow Instagram access to your Contacts. This is your last chance to cancel your decision to allow Instagram to access your contacts.

6. **Tap OK.**

   The pop-up goes away, and the Contacts screen appears, as shown in Figure 7-2.

7. **Follow all your contacts on Instagram by tapping Follow All, or choose which contacts to follow by tapping Follow next to each one.**

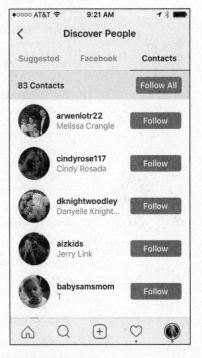

FIGURE 7-2:
Instagram can pull contacts from your phone's saved contacts for you to select to follow.

If you change your mind at some point and want to disallow Instagram's access to your contacts, tap the wheel icon on your profile page, scroll down to Settings, and then tap Contacts. Tap the Connect Contacts toggle to return it to white, which terminates Instagram's access.

Finding New Friends

Now that you've found all your Facebook friends and contacts on Instagram, it's time to get more strategic about following the people who might have a genuine interest in your business. Instagram offers several options for exploring, searching, and suggesting new followers to you.

Exploring the Explore function

Instagram loves growth . . . the more people you engage with, the more users they get. And to keep those people, Instagram offers many ways to engage with them. One way is through the Explore page. The Explore page offers photo, graphic, and video posts that Instagram thinks might be interesting to you. No one knows the exact algorithm, but they usually present a variety of posts that have received at least 1,000 likes mixed in with posts that other people you follow have liked.

Here's how to use the Explore page:

1. **Tap the magnifying glass at the bottom of any screen.**

   Several photos, videos, and stories are presented, as shown in Figure 7-3.

   TIP

   If you're trying to get your posts displayed on the Explore page, note that the Instagram algorithm rarely selects graphics such as charts or infographs. It tends to favor photos or videos.

2. **Tap any photo or video that interests you.**

   Now you can scroll down to see the rest of the Explore page.

3. **Tap the Instagram username at the top of any post that interests you.**

4. **Look around the page. If you like what you see:**

   a. *Like one or more photos: Double-tap each individual photo or tap the heart icon.*

FIGURE 7-3:
The Explore page displays stories, videos, and posts you might like.

b. *Leave a comment: Tap the photo, and then tap the comment bubble below the photo. Enter your text, and tap the blue Post link.*

c. *To follow a user: Tap the blue Follow button at the top of the user's profile page.*

After you follow this page, Instagram offers several other accounts that it thinks you'd enjoy following. We detail this method of finding accounts to follow in the "Letting Instagram suggest users to you" section, later in this chapter.

TIP

This method of finding followers is time consuming. Also, popular accounts may not be looking to follow many new people, so there's no guarantee that you'll get a reciprocal follow. However, it's always worth a shot and is a nice addition to your follower strategy.

Searching the Search feature

Another great way to find new accounts to follow is through searching Instagram. Instagram offers four ways to search: Top, People, Tags, and Places.

To try out the Search feature, tap the magnifying glass on any page. The Explore page appears, as described in the preceding section. Tap the Search field at the top of the page. Top, People, Tags, and Places are now available for your choosing, as shown in Figure 7-4.

The *Top feature* shows you accounts that you interact with often, followed by accounts you most recently interacted with. To find new followers, search for an industry or a keyword that relates to your business or target customer. For instance, typing **real estate** presents several accounts that have *real estate* in their username or in their profile title. Scroll through those that are interesting, and follow those you like!

The *People feature* can be used in a similar manner to the Top feature, but you may also choose to search by someone's name. If you have a customer list, try searching for people by name. For those that pop up, scroll

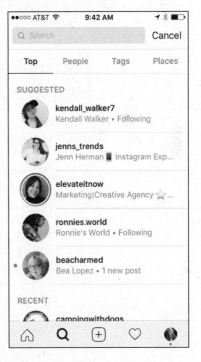

FIGURE 7-4:
Search by Top, People, Tags, and Places.

through to their account and follow them if they seem to be active. Personal accounts are more likely to be private, so you will need to request access.

The *Tags feature* allows you to search by hashtag. Start simply by choosing your industry and see what appears. For example, if you're a dog trainer, start with #dogtraining. If you get too many results to be useful, add your city or state, such as #dogtrainingsacramento. Scroll through the accounts and tap the ones that call out to you. Then follow the ones that seem active and engaging. In the next chapter, hashtags are discussed in detail, and we explain more about this feature.

The *Places feature* enables you to search by location. If you're currently near your business location, the easiest way to start is to tap Near Current Location. Several nearby locations then pop up for your choosing. Tap a location near you, and then all the posts that marked that location on their post pop up. Tap some posts that catch your eye, and follow the ones you like.

On all the accounts you follow, make sure to like several posts and leave a meaningful comment or two (not just an emoji). This technique greatly increases the odds that the account will follow you back.

Letting Instagram suggest users to you

As mentioned, Instagram is on a mission to grow. Therefore, its main goal is making its users happy by making their accounts grow. When you follow someone, an algorithm kicks in and displays other similar accounts that you may like following. In Figure 7-5, we decide to follow @elevateitnow, a marketing and creative agency. Instagram then presents many other social-media-marketing business accounts, and we can decide whether or not to follow them.

You might be wondering why you'd want to follow. They might not follow you back (but they will if they're smart). In the next section, you learn more about the benefits of keeping tabs on the competition.

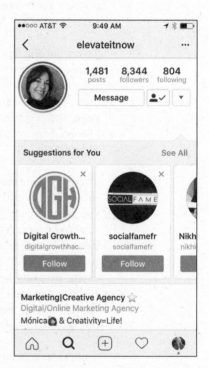

FIGURE 7-5:
After you follow an account, Instagram presents similar accounts you might like.

Following Your Industry

Watching your industry's Instagram accounts can help you build your following in several ways. In this section, you find out how to benefit from the earlier work of your competitors and industry icons. First, if your business serves only local customers, look at your direct, local competition. Then look more globally at bigger brands in the same industry to see the tactics they use.

Following industry hashtags is also highly productive. Does your industry hold several large conferences a year? Conferences are usually associated with a hashtag. Savvy Instagram business accounts incorporate the conference hashtag in their posts so consider searching for the hashtag to find other accounts to interact with. These accounts could be competitors or potential customers. If you're attending the event, search through the conference hashtag and follow accounts, like photos, comment, and perhaps direct message other attendees to set in-person meetings with potential customers or business partners.

Watching your competition

One of the best ways to find new followers is by researching your competitors' Instagram accounts and interacting with their followers. If they're interested in your competitor's business, they might be interested in your offerings as well. Your competitors' follower lists are like a ready-made target audience waiting just for you!

Engaging with your competitors' followers is easy. Here's how:

1. **Make a list of your top competitors.**

2. **Use the Search function to find one of them on Instagram.**

   For details on searching, see the "Searching the Search feature" section, earlier in the chapter.

3. **Go to a competitor's account, and tap the number above *followers* (at the top right of its profile page).**

   In Figure 7-6, the followers number is 2,615.

   You see everyone following the competitor, as shown in Figure 7-7.

4. **Do the following for each follower account that looks interesting:**

   a. *Tap the account.*

   b. *Like several photos and comment on at least one post.*

   c. *Follow the account.*

5. **Repeat Steps 3 and 4 for all the competitors in your list.**

Keep regularly engaging with these accounts, and you might just win them over to following you or becoming a customer.

FIGURE 7-6:
You can see a competitor's followers by tapping its number of followers.

FIGURE 7-7:
Tap your competitor's follower accounts to decide if you'd like to follow them.

Getting noticed by big brands

Following big brands such as Target, Maybelline, or Yoplait provides unique ideas for content or promotions done in a fresh way, but it can also yield more followers for you. How? Some big brands re-post user-generated content (content created by regular folks like you and us) from their customers, and when they do, that account can hit the jackpot on followers.

To get noticed by a big brand, follow these tips:

1. Make a list of top brands that would mesh well with your brand. For example, if you sell virtual assistant services, you might make a list of various companies that sell planners, specialty pens, and desk accessories.

2. Check whether the company re-posts images from other users by scrolling through several months of posts. Some companies are strict about their brand, and post only what has been designed by their design department. If this is the case, cross them off the list.

3. After you find a brand that does re-post user-generated content, study the posts it shares from other accounts. Do they typically like flat lays (photos where products are neatly arranged on a background and photographed from above); photos with people, animals, or sports; a consistent filter? You might notice a pattern in what has been selected. Put your own flair on your content while making it fit the other account's style.

4. Style your photo according to the instructions in Step 3, and include the company's product with the brand label prominently displayed. Do not include other brands in the photo.

5. Add brand hashtags. Big brands often have a specific hashtag they associate with all their posts. For example, Coca-Cola uses #ShareaCoke as its branded hashtag on Instagram posts. If you're trying to get featured on @Cocacola, use the #ShareaCoke hashtag along with other hashtags that relate to the soda brand.

6. Mention the brand using its Instagram username in your written post. For instance, @coreycwalker used the hashtag #madeonterra in a post where she used the brand's cupcake toppers in a photo. She was then featured on the @madeonterra Instagram page and was tagged back. Now @madeonterra followers might visit @coreycwalker's page to see what else she posts. See Figure 7-8 for the post featured on the @madeonterra account.

© Made on Terra

FIGURE 7-8:
Sometimes brands re-post user-generated content like this one by @madeonterra.

Deciding Whom to Follow Back

After you've employed the techniques described previously in this chapter, you'll begin to get more followers. It's a great feeling to see that number go up on your profile page, and your next decision is whether to follow those accounts back if you were not already following them. In this next section, you discover how to view your followers and decide who is best to follow back.

Viewing and following your followers

So you are starting to see more followers on your account. Now it's time to learn a simple method to follow them back. You're not required or even expected to follow someone back, but searching through your followers often yields great customer prospects. New followers appear in your notifications, but if you don't check your notifications often, it's worth checking out your follower list every few days to see whom you might want to follow back.

Checking your follower list is easy:

1. **Go to your profile page and click the number above *followers*.**

   All of your followers appear, with the most recent followers at the top. As shown in Figure 7-9, followers you have not followed back have a blue Follow button to the right that you can click to follow. If you're already following them, it says Following.

2. **Unless you recognize the username, click that name to view the user's profile page.**

3. **If you think that the user is a potential customer or partner, click the blue Follow button on his or her profile page. Otherwise, use the arrow on the top left of the page to go back to your follower list and try again.**

4. **Like a few posts and leave a meaningful comment.**

   In this way, the follower is more likely to engage with you in the future.

FIGURE 7-9:
Followers you haven't followed back have a blue Follow button to the right.

Reciprocating a follow or not

Now that you know a simple method for following back, the question is whether the account is worthy of following back. Some accounts have a habit of following accounts but then unfollowing them if they didn't follow back. You might see your numbers rise by 25, just to fall back by 22 the next day. It's a frustrating game that you should avoid.

Do follow back the following:

> » Accounts of friends, local businesses, and other people you know and like in real life (or as the kids say, "IRL")

> » Accounts in your industry, especially competitors! If they're checking up on you, it's wise to see what they're doing

> » Accounts of businesses you do business with or other related associates

> » Accounts that provide content inspiration, even if they're not in your industry

> » Accounts of people you have met on other networks, such as Facebook groups, Twitter, or LinkedIn

> » Accounts that you find personally interesting and satisfying to view and interact with, even if they're not directly tied to your business

Not every account you follow back needs to be your ultimate moneymaker. Instagram is still meant to be fun; it doesn't have to be dry and boring, even if your business is unexciting. Plus, you never know who is a friend of a friend or a cousin of someone who could be an amazing connection. Connecting with others on Instagram could be the first step in a business match made in heaven!

Don't follow back:

> » Everyone who follows you because you feel some sort of obligation.

> » Spammy accounts whose profile probably lists only a few posts and who often sell follower services.

> » Accounts that use bots to leave automated comments. (Nothing is worse than having someone write "Love it!" when you post that your dog just died.)

> » Accounts that contain content you have no interest in personally or professionally.

> » Accounts that follow you for a few days, then unfollow you, and then follow you again a week later. They often use the #follow4follow hashtag. Stay away!

TIP

You may discover your own rules for following accounts. Keep in mind that it's okay to unfollow people too. Maybe they stopped posting, or their content no longer interests you. Clean up your feed every so often to ensure that you're viewing the best content for you and your business.

Finding Your Insta-Tribe

If you compare all the popular social networks — Facebook, Twitter, LinkedIn, Snapchat, and Instagram — the one that takes the cake on community engagement is Instagram. This section explains how to use hashtags influencers, interaction, and Instagram pods to find your ultimate Insta-tribe!

Finding or creating a community you vibe with

If you've been on Instagram for a while, you've probably seen posts talking about community and finding your tribe. But what does that mean? A *community,* or *tribe,* is a supportive group of people talking about and interacting with you and your brand on Instagram. They offer advice, give a heads up about changes on Instagram or your industry, provide support, promote your business when it makes sense, and leave comments that can help boost your posts. If executed well, your community is marketing gold.

Your first step is finding a community that fits with your brand. An easy way to do this is through hashtags. If you sell high-end baby dresses, for example, searching #baby yields several other relevant hashtags such as #babyshower, #babygirl, #babybump, #babyboy, #babybrother, and #babyshoes.

All of these hashtags are large, so by selecting one and creating a new search (as shown in Figure 7-10), you can find more specific

FIGURE 7-10:
Search hashtags to see Instagram's suggestions of other more specific hashtags.

hashtags, such as #babygirlstuff, #babygirlnation, #babygirlootd, and #babygirl-fashion. Search for people who use these niche hashtags often. Then follow them and interact with them daily by commenting and liking their posts.

While you're commenting on their posts, you'll probably start seeing other people showing up frequently on the same accounts. Follow, like, and comment on those accounts too, and before you know it, your tribe is developing!

To further solidify your relationship, send them a quick direct message to introduce yourself and your business. (Direct messages are covered in Chapter 6.) Because you're just meeting, it's not the time to make a sales pitch. Let the relationship flow naturally and tell them how much you enjoy the conversations you've had.

After you're in a community, certain influencers and brands may bubble to the surface. These accounts are excellent to interact with because the audience you're trying to reach sees them often. Leaving meaningful or humorous comments regularly on an influencer or a big brand account can help your following and can lead to a relationship with that influencer or brand.

You may also find your tribe completely away from Instagram. For example, Facebook groups catering to niche markets often have Instagram tribes that coincide with the group. They might have their own unique hashtags to easily identify them on Instagram. You may also discover them by following the admin of the group, and seeing the same people interacting on Instagram.

Not finding the tribe you're seeking? Start your own! Run a contest or campaign asking people to submit a photo that goes with your hashtag. For example, if you're a graphic designer, you could start a challenge using #graphicdesignotd, where designers post what they worked on that day. People love challenges like this because it provides post inspiration and an excuse to show off their work! Keep checking the hashtag for submissions, and thank everyone for participating. Then follow them, and keep coming back regularly, commenting and liking their posts. All of a sudden, a tribe is forming!

REMEMBER

With any of these methods for finding or creating your tribe, the most important element is engagement. By liking and commenting often, you get the same in return. Tribe members get to know each other on a deeper level by watching for those special posts every day. The friendships can lead to business connections, conference buddies, and more. Like the old saying goes: The more you give, the more you get back!

Deciding whether Instagram pods are beneficial

When Instagram changed from displaying posts chronologically to using an algorithm based on users' likes to show posts, many marketers panicked. It seemed like Facebook all over again — pushing people toward advertising to get their posts shown. To combat this, many savvy marketers turned to Instagram pods. A *pod* is a group of 10 to 20 accounts that usually have something in common. Maybe they're all photographers, or DIY crafters, or mommy bloggers. They all have the main goal of getting more engagement.

This is how a pod works:

>> Instagrammers recruit several other accounts via Instagram DM (direct message) or a Facebook group. (See Chapter 6 for details on direct messaging.)

>> The people in the pod post their content on Instagram, and then share that post via a group DM set up for the pod members, as shown in Figure 7-11.

>> Pod members then click through to the person's Instagram account, liking and commenting on the post as soon as possible to help boost the post in Instagram's algorithm. Likes and comments within the first hour of a post do the most work to get a post shown more often in Instagram feeds.

>> Pod members have a responsibility to engage as often and as quickly as possible on other pod members' posts to boost engagement. Some people find the responsibility overwhelming, particularly if members of the pod post several times a day.

FIGURE 7-11:
Pod members share their posts with other members via direct message.

Does it work? Is it worth the time? The data is not clear. If you have an active group, the comments should help your engagement and likes somewhat. However, participating in a pod can be a huge time commitment and can leave you feeling tethered to your phone waiting for the next post. It's hard to run a business that way.

Often people join a pod, use it for a while, form a few good friendships, and then break up at some point due to the time commitment. You may find your Insta-tribe during this process and still interact with the same accounts from your pod after the breakup but without the pressure of commenting on-demand.

TIP

If you'd like to try a pod, start small, with no more than 15 accounts. If you like the results and can keep up, try a larger one. However, your pod should never detract from your larger audience. If you find that you have time to comment on only the same few accounts in your pod, it's best to let the pod go and get back to interacting with your audience as a whole.

» Following the rules of hashtags for great results

» Finding which hashtags are the best for your brand

» Creating hashtags for your brand, contest, or promotion

Chapter **8**

Wielding the Power of the Hashtag

You are starting to create cool content and have followed many people, but for some reason, your photos are garnering only a few likes. Want a solution to this problem? The answer is hashtags. Hashtags give your posts more reach by making them searchable to anyone, not just those in your immediate network. In fact, a study by Simply Measured (www.simplymeasured.com) found that adding just one hashtag to Instagram posts yielded an average 12.6 percent increase in engagement (likes and comments).

In this chapter, you learn how to place hashtags and discover the best practices of using hashtags. You also find out how to research hashtags that apply to your business and create branded hashtags for your Instagram account. If you're interested in learning about hashtags for Instagram Stories, we suggest getting the basics about hashtags here first and then reading Chapters 9 and 10.

Investigating Hashtags

To get started, we discuss what hashtags are and why it's important to use them on Instagram. Hashtags always start with the # sign (found on the bottom right of your mobile phone keyboard when typing, or by pressing Shift-3 on a desktop computer keyboard) followed by a word, a phrase, a number, or an emoji with no spaces, such as #sundayvibes or #instamood.

REMEMBER

Characters such as $ and % as well as periods and underscores do not work in hashtags.

To add a hashtag to your photo, image, or video, follow these instructions:

1. **Take or upload a photo, image, or video. Tap Next.**

2. **Add a filter if you want. Tap Next.**

3. **Type or copy and paste your caption in the Write a Caption field.**

4. **Add hashtags using one of the following methods:**

   - Before you share your post: *Type or cut and paste up to 30 hashtags after your text in the caption, as shown in Figure 8-1, left, and then tap Share at the top right of the screen.*

   - After you've shared your post: *Tap the Comment bubble, and type or cut and paste up to 30 hashtags in the comment field, as shown in Figure 8-1, right. Tap Post.*

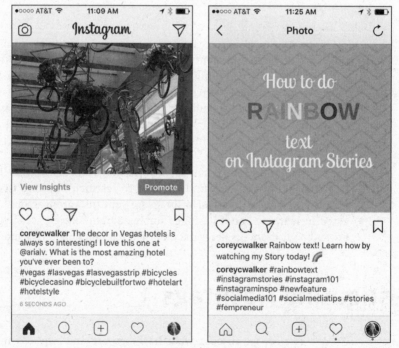

FIGURE 8-1: Hashtags can go in the caption (left) or below the caption in the comments (right).

TIP

No functional difference exists between placing your hashtags in the caption or in the comments. Which method you use is your personal preference.

After you add a hashtag to your caption or comment, the hashtag becomes a searchable link that takes you to a page of all the posts using that hashtag (a *hashtag hub*) when tapped. Figure 8-2 shows the hashtag hub for #bicyclebuiltfortwo.

Hashtags are added to a hashtag hub chronologically, based on when the photo was posted, not when the hashtag posts. Going back days later and adding hashtags to a post will not bump your post back up in the hashtag hub.

People search hashtags to find content for a variety of reasons, such as to find a product, to learn how to do something, to follow a brand, or even to watch videos of a certain theme. We go over how to search hashtags later, in the "Researching the Right Hashtags" section.

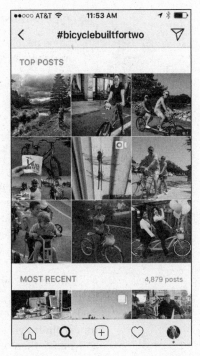

FIGURE 8-2:
When you tap a hashtag, you see a page with other recent posts that use that hashtag.

TIP

If you have a private account, only users who are your approved followers will see your posts, even with a hashtag. If you're trying to get a wider audience, set your account to public so anyone can search for your content via hashtags.

Following Hashtag Best Practices

Hashtags seem simple enough, right? But there's more to them than meets the eye, and any serious Instagrammer will tell you to follow certain do's and don'ts when using hashtags. In this section, we detail best practices for using hashtags.

Placing hashtags so you don't annoy people

If you're familiar with using hashtags on Facebook or Twitter, you're probably used to putting a couple of hashtags directly in your post. On Instagram, however, you can use up to 30 hashtags in a caption. Use one of the following tactics to keep your captions uncluttered:

TIP

>> **Type hashtags after the text in your caption.** Refer to Figure 8-1, left.

   Some people type period, return, period, return several times to move the hashtags farther down out of the way of the caption text.

>> **Place hashtags in the comment directly below your caption.** Refer to Figure 8-1, right.

Knowing how many hashtags are best

Although Instagram allows 30 hashtags per post, some studies report that using that many hashtags looks spammy and do not advise the practice. See Figure 8-3 for an example.

A study done by TrackMaven (https://trackmaven.com/resources/hashtag-best-practices/) looked at hashtag usage for accounts with 1,000 or fewer followers and found that 9 to 12 hashtags were the optimal amount to get the most engagement. After 12 hashtags, engagement dropped off. That said, see what works for your account by trying varying amounts of hashtags and logging the results.

WARNING

If you use more than 30 hashtags in a caption or a comment on your post, Instagram will not post the accompanying photo or video. Make sure to count all hashtags you use, especially if you use one or two in your caption and then a full list in a comment below to ensure that your photo or video will post.

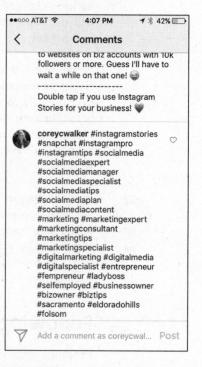

FIGURE 8-3:
This many hashtags can look spammy.

TIP

The TrackMaven study also found that longer hashtags perform better than short ones. The optimal character length for a hashtag was 21 characters. With 25 or more characters, engagement quickly declined.

Popular hashtags and when to use them

Believe it or not, hashtags, just like students in high school, can be popular and not so popular. There are good reasons to use some of both hashtag types. In addition, you should avoid some hashtags.

Here are some popular hashtags:

» #beautiful

» #cute

» #fashion

» #happy

» #instagood

» #love

» #me

» #photooftheday

» #picoftheday

» #selfie

» #tbt

Although these hashtags are seen by a large population on the hashtag hub (but probably not your target audience), the post may be shown for only a few moments. Those hashtags are used by millions of people daily, so they're quickly replaced by the next post using that hashtag.

When Instagram's algorithm detects a popular post (with quick engagement), it appears in the Top Posts section at the top of the hashtag hub (see Figure 8-4). These posts stay up longer. Top Posts is a coveted position because it is the first thing anyone sees when searching a hashtag. It's also a badge of honor because the best performing posts are shown there.

FIGURE 8-4:
The Top Posts area displays the most popular posts using a particular hashtag.

The popular hashtags should be used only if they apply to your post. Throwing a bunch of hashtags that don't apply to your photo or video may get it seen briefly, but it's a bad practice because people searching that hashtag won't find what they're looking for and might be ticked off that you used it.

An unlimited number of hashtags are available, and many will perform much better for you than popular hashtags because they're more specific to your business. For instance, a solar company might choose #solar, #solarenergy, #solarpanels, #renewableenergy, #poweredbythesun, #savemoneyandenergy, #renewables, #sunpowered, and #saynotofossilfuels.

One effective tactic is to mix hashtags that receive a lot of traffic with hashtags that get little traffic. With this method, your post is seen briefly right away by many people searching for the popular hashtags. Meanwhile, your less popular hashtags are seen by fewer (yet more targeted) people for a longer time and have a better chance of making it into Top Posts. Your post may even stay there for a few days! We discuss how to research hashtags later in the section, "Researching the Right Hashtags."

TIP

You should avoid some popular hashtags, such as any that encourage following (#follow, #follow4follow, #followforfollow, #followforlikes, #followme). People who have no interest in your business will end up following and then unfollowing you. It's a big waste of time. Hashtags that reference sexual activity or body parts are generally blocked too, and don't normally belong on a business post anyway.

Storing hashtags for later

If you plan on using hashtags regularly, typing them into your phone by hand will quickly become tedious. Following are a few work-arounds for this problem:

>> **Notes:** The Notes app is preloaded on iPhones, and similar apps like ColorNote or Evernote are available for download on Android phones. Create a new note for different categories or products, and then list up to 30 hashtags, as shown in Figure 8-5, left. Before you tap Share on your post, go over to your note and copy the desired hashtags. Tap Share and open a comment to paste the hashtags.

>> **Email:** Another easy solution is to email yourself lists of hashtags. Simply open a new email, use the hashtag category in the Subject line, and then type up to 30 hashtags, as shown in Figure 8-5, middle. Create several emails with different hashtag lists, and then store them in a special email folder to retrieve and cut and paste quickly and easily.

>> **Tailwind:** A complete all-in-one solution, the Tailwind app (see Figure 8-5, right) offers hashtag saving, plus content management for Instagram

and Pinterest. You can upload your content, schedule it, get hashtag suggestions, save hashtag lists for later, and measure analytics. Unlike the Notes app or email, Tailwind is not free. Accounts including hashtag saving start at $9.99 a month.

FIGURE 8-5: Store hashtags in a notes app (left), an email message (middle), or the Tailwind app.

TIP

If you regularly string together the same hashtags, use predictive text on your phone to populate a set of hashtags. That way, you won't need to store them in a separate location.

Tracking hashtag analytics

If you'd like in-depth reporting about which hashtags are performing best for you, many apps can help. The three most popular apps for hashtag analytics follow:

» **Iconosquare** (https://pro.iconosquare.com): This all-in-one app can not only monitor hashtag performance but also serve as your content management system to store, schedule, and post content. For hashtags specifically, you can see how each hashtag you use affects engagement (as shown in Figure 8-6); discover your most influential posts by hashtag; view the most influential people using a particular hashtag; and see the location of most of the people who are viewing a hashtag. Iconosquare tracks Instagram only and starts at $261/year if you include the hashtag-tracking features.

FIGURE 8-6: Iconosquare offers several ways to track hashtag analytics.

© Iconosquare

>> **Sprout Social** (`https://sproutsocial.com`): Sprout Social's Instagram integration includes scheduling, engagement tools, and access to rich analytics. Using Sprout's all-in-one platform you can plan content and post to your Instagram profile, respond to comments on your posts, and monitor and engage with people. You can also see your outbound hashtag performance, which rates your most used hashtags and your most engaged hashtags, as shown in Figure 8-7. Finally, you can search hashtags to see campaign results for contests that collect user-generated content tagged with your branded hashtag. Sprout Social is a robust solution and starts at $99/month.

>> **Tailwind:** Tailwind is a content management system tailored to Instagram and Pinterest only. It provides many ways to track hashtags, including the following: daily activity, engagement, and trends (see Figure 8-8); popular topics and hashtags related to your brand; which photos are getting the most likes and comments by hashtag; where hashtags are working better geographically; and suggestions for related hashtags to use. Unfortunately, these features are available only at the Enterprise level (price not listed), which may be more than you want to spend if you're a small-business owner.

As you can see, hashtag analytics apps are available, but they often require an investment. Start using Instagram and decide how closely you'll be monitoring hashtags, and then decide whether an analytic app is worth the expense.

Outbound Hashtag Performance

MOST USED HASHTAGS		MOST ENGAGED HASHTAGS	
#freshlyground	44	#cafe	93
#espresso	23	#coffee	84
#cafe	20	#espresso	78
#latte	18	#chicago	15
#darkroast	16	#slomo	9
#coffee	14	#artinstitute	9
#chicago	13	#caffeine	9
#creamandsugar	13	#coffeeandthecup	9
#jumpstart	11	#foodporn	8
#tillthelastdrop	10	#sothirsty	8

FIGURE 8-7:
Sprout Social can display your most used and most engaged hashtags.

© Sprout Social

FIGURE 8-8:
Tailwind offers several in-depth hashtag analytics, but only at the Enterprise level.

Researching the Right Hashtags

You've been given the best practices about where to put, store, and analyze hashtags, but how can you find the right ones? In this section, we discuss several ways to research hashtags for your posts, including checking out the competition, finding related hashtags, and looking at influencer hashtags.

Checking out the competition

If you're looking for robust competitive hashtag analysis, Iconosquare and Sprout Social offer tools to dive into the competition's hashtags for a price. A free app that will let you search hashtags and easily see the results on a dashboard is Tagboard (www.tagboard.com). You can also search hashtags quickly using Instagram itself as detailed next.

Follow these steps to research your competitors' hashtags:

1. **Create a list of your top competitors, including their Instagram username, in Excel or another spreadsheet program.**

   Create a spreadsheet with columns for competitor names and hashtags. You can also include product or service categories if that makes sense for your business. See Figure 8-9 for an example. (This process is detailed in Chapter 7 in the section about watching your competition.)

	A	B	C	D
1	**Competitor Hashtags**			
2	**Competitor**	**Category**	**Hashtags**	**High Likes**
3	Bob's Grocery	Vegetables	#summersbest #locallygrown #organic #organicveggies #pesticidefree #tomatoes #broccoli #lettuce	Y
4				
5				

2. **Log in to your Instagram account on your desktop by going to www.instagram.com/*username* and entering your username and password.**

   You must access Instagram on your desktop computer because you can't copy and paste your competitor's hashtags from your mobile device.

3. **Refer to your competitor list and type a username in the Search box at the top of the Instagram screen.**

4. **Click one of the competitor's images, and view the hashtags.**

   Copy and paste the hashtags into the Excel spreadsheet.

5. **Go through at least five images, copying and pasting any new hashtags you find.**

   Note on the spreadsheet any images that received a lot of likes. You won't be able to tell if the image's popularity is due to the image or the hashtags, but include the information just in case.

6. **Repeat Steps 3–5 for all competitors on your list.**

   Compare hashtags that they're all using, and add them to your business's hashtag list. Also note hashtags on posts in which multiple competitors received a lot of likes.

7. **Go to your Instagram mobile app and get more information about the popularity or the hashtags in your list:**

   a. *Tap the magnifying glass at the bottom of your Instagram app screen, and then tap inside the Search box.*

   b. *On the next page that appears, tap Tags.*

   c. *Enter one of the hashtags from your competitor list.* The hashtag you entered will appear first, with the number of posts that have used it, plus other related hashtags and how often they've been used.

   Use this information to mix some high-use and low-use hashtags, increasing the chance that your post will be seen.

REMEMBER

Manual tracking is not an exact science, but it will expose you to new hashtags. And you might find a hashtag that propels the views to your account.

Picking up on related hashtags

You can find related hashtags for your business in a number of ways. One easy method using Instagram mobile is to tap any hashtag you've already used on one of your posts. That hashtag hub appears, with related hashtags shown at the top. For example, Figure 8-10 shows the hashtag #mompreneur.

You can also search other hashtags by tapping the magnifying glass at the bottom of your Instagram profile, typing a hashtag in the Search field at the top of the screen, and tapping Search.

Two additional free resources for related hashtags are RiteTag (www.ritetag.com) and Hashtagify (www.hashtagify.me). With RiteTag, shown in Figure 8-11, you enter a hashtag, and it generates other suggested hashtags. It separates the hashtags into hot now hashtags, which are seen quickly (and go away quickly), hashtags that are seen over time, and hashtags to avoid because no one is viewing them. RiteTag is a handy tool!

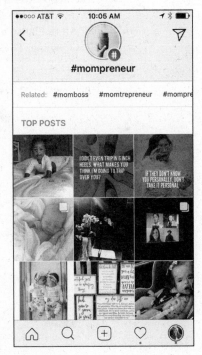

FIGURE 8-10:
Instagram offers suggested related hashtags in the mobile app.

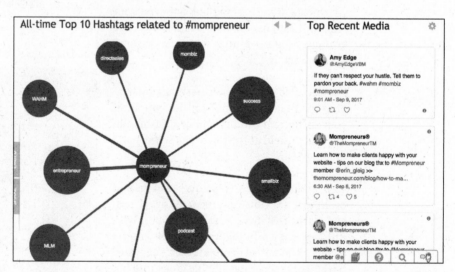

FIGURE 8-11:
RiteTag ranks
suggested
hashtags for you
by hot now, seen
over time, and
avoid using.

When you enter a hashtag in Hashtagify, it generates a fun spoke-wheel visual of the all-time top-ten related hashtags for the word or phrase you entered, as shown in Figure 8-12. You also see recent posts by other accounts that have used that hashtag. These might be good competitors to watch!

FIGURE 8-12:
Hashtagify
displays the top
10 hashtags
related to the
hashtag you
entered.

Whether you use Instagram's hashtag suggestions, RiteTag or Hashtagify, make sure you store the results. You can use a simple Excel spreadsheet or one of the methods described earlier, in the "Storing hashtags for later" section.

Discovering what the cool kids are doing (influencer hashtags)

Another way to find great hashtags is to research what the influencers for your industry are using. *Influencers* are key people that your target audience follows and whose opinions are highly regarded. Most industries have a few key people who are popular and widely followed. If you don't know who those people are, follow these steps to find them:

1. **Choose one of the hashtags that you or a competitor uses that is specific to your business.**

   For example, choose #sandiegorestaurant instead of #restaurant.

2. **Do a Google search of that hashtag.**

   For example, in Figure 8-13, we typed *#sandiegorestaurant on instagram*.

3. **Click through to the posts that appear on Instagram. If a username is frequently featured:**

   a. *Note the username, and check to see how the number of likes and how many followers the account has.*

   b. *If the username seems like a good influencer for your industry, write down some of the other hashtags the account is using to reach your audience. Add these hashtags to your saved hashtag lists.*

FIGURE 8-13: Searching for a popular hashtag can reveal influencers who may have more hashtag ideas for you.

Creating a Branded Hashtag

Surely you've seen the hashtag #YesWeCan, or #ShareaCoke, right? These are examples of branded hashtags. A branded hashtag may start as a campaign slogan and then morph over to easily become a branded hashtag. But sometimes it's not that simple, and you'll need to do more research before launching a branded hashtag.

Here are the steps for creating a branded hashtag for your business:

1. Start by making a list of all hashtags that relate to your brand, including any slogans you use regularly.

2. Search that hashtag on Twitter and Instagram to make sure it's not already being used by someone else or for something unsavory.

3. Share the hashtag with several people to see ensure that it makes sense and the letters don't run together to form new words. For instance, the ill-fated hashtag for Kids Exchange, a consignment store for kids' clothes, was #kidsexchange, which could be misread as "kid sex change."

4. Use the hashtag on your Instagram posts (and other social media), Power Point presentations, flyers, ads, and packaging to get people accustomed to seeing it and using it to tag their posts about your product or service.

Branded hashtags offer an easy way for followers to search for their favorite brands on Instagram. After you have true fans, they'll start using your hashtag on their posts, to showcase your product or service in their post or simply to interact with you. Be sure to check your branded hashtag often so you can respond and react to posts that include it!

In the next two sections, you discover best practices for using a hashtag for a promotion or contest, and how to gather user-generated content through hashtags.

REMEMBER

As documented in a study by TrackMaven, a longer hashtag (21 to 24 characters) is better, but make sure it's something that is easy to remember and spell. Don't use weird abbreviations or terms that people might find confusing.

Hashtag your promotion or contest

If you're launching a promotion or contest, it's important to use a unique hashtag so you can easily follow the activity of users interacting with you. (See Chapter 13 for details on setting up an Instagram contest from start to finish.)

If you already have a branded hashtag for your business, you should choose a new hashtag for this promotion or contest only. Follow the guidelines just mentioned for creating a branded hashtag, but make it specific to this contest. If your branded hashtag has already gone viral, you could just add *contest* to the end of it, such as #JustDoItContest, to capitalize on your already known brand.

Start using the hashtag on all posts, material, and websites related to the promotion or contest. Give followers instructions for using the hashtag in their posts, as shown in Figure 8-14.

After your promotion or contest is underway, check the hashtag often (by tapping it) to monitor the conversation or gather contest entries or both. Another simple way to view hashtags is to tap the magnifying glass at the bottom of your Instagram mobile app, and then type the hashtag in the Search box. A page with just those hashtags will appear, as shown in Figure 8-15, for you to view, respond to, and collect as contest entries.

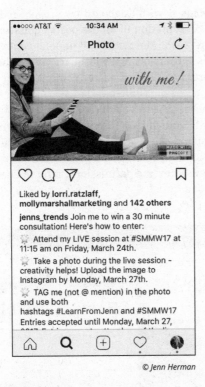

© Jenn Herman

FIGURE 8-14:
@jenns_trends tells followers that they can enter her contest by using the hashtags #LearnFromJenn and #SMMW17 in their entry posts.

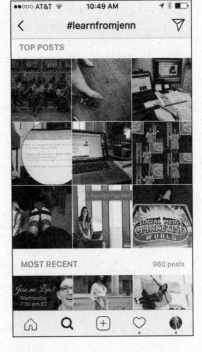

FIGURE 8-15:
Search results for the hashtag #learnfromjenn.

Gathering user-generated content

When you're running a promotion or contest, you might ask followers to submit a piece of their own content to enter the contest. In Figure 8-14, for example, @jenns_trends tells her followers to take a photo during her live conference session and upload the image by Monday.

User-generated content paired with your promotion or contest hashtag is an excellent way to expand the reach of your promotion or contest. The followers who submit content are now spreading the hashtag among their followers. Depending on the size of your brand or how viral the contest, this method can increase your reach exponentially.

Check the hashtag by tapping the magnifying glass at the bottom of your Instagram mobile app, and then typing the hashtag in the Search area. Refer to Figure 8-15 for an example of what the results look like.

Another way to track hashtags is with Tagboard (www.tagboard.com). This app gives a more easily viewed presentation of all the posts submitted with a certain hashtag, as shown in Figure 8-16. Most other all-in-one content-management systems we describe, such as Sprout Social, Iconosquare, and Tailwind, also enable you to search for your hashtags to view submitted content.

Finally, after you find the user-generated content via your hashtag, repost it or notify the winner or both! If your initial instructions did not include a phrase about the follower granting permission to use the image as a condition of submitting it, make sure you contact the person to get permission to repost. For official language about contest submissions and permissions, refer to Chapter 13's section on defining rules or conditions.

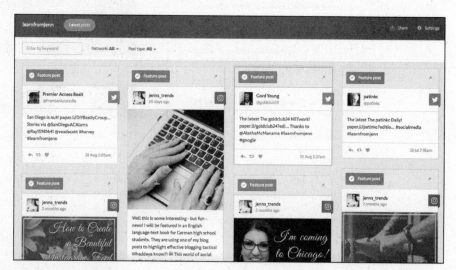

FIGURE 8-16: Use Tagboard to search and view user-generated content easily.

4

Making Your Garden Grow

Share and advertise your Instagram Stories.

Create a winning Instagram ad for your business.

Test your ad and get insights about its popularity on Instagram and Facebook.

Produce a winning Instagram contest to bring fun to your followers.

Mix your Instagram profile into your social marketing recipe.

Chapter 9

Sharing with Instagram Stories

Throughout this book, we discuss many features in Instagram's original newsfeed. But did you know that the Instagram mobile app also has a completely different section called Instagram Stories?

Instagram Stories were introduced in the latter half of 2016 in an attempt to get more users to post content. The lure was that the content disappears within 24 hours, allowing those that had been meticulously curating their semi-permanent Instagram feed to hang loose a bit. Users now have a place on Instagram where they can be more spontaneous, by, say, taking a quick behind-the-scenes photo or shooting a 15-second video explaining something they did that day.

In this chapter, you learn all about Instagram Stories and discover which type of content is best. In the next chapter, you find out about enhancements you can add to your Stories.

Instagram Stories are a great complement to your regular Instagram feed, so don't skip out on this chapter!

Checking Out Instagram Stories

Before you start creating your own Story, it's helpful to learn about how Instagram Stories started and watch a few Stories others have created.

It's no secret that Instagram Stories are a copycat of Snapchat's Stories; Instagram didn't even bother to change the name! Snapchat was garnering a lot of growth and success with its Stories, particularly in the teens and twenties demographic. Instagram (and its daddy, Facebook) took the feature that most people liked best about Snapchat — Stories — and built it into Instagram. The addition of Stories and their fun filters (although not as robust as Snapchat's), added to Instagram's explosive growth.

Now that we have the short history of Instagram Stories out of the way, let's talk about where to find them. Instagram Stories are located in a bar at the top of your newsfeed and are represented by a multicolored ring around the profile picture of the Story's creator, as shown in Figure 9-1, left. Tap the profile picture, and the Story opens full-screen. Unlike on a regular posts, you can't like or comment publicly. You can, however, send a direct message, as shown in Figure 9-1, right.

FIGURE 9-1:
View Stories by tapping a profile picture at the top of your newsfeed (left). Stories open up full-screen on your phone (right).

New Stories (personalized for you) are shown first. By scrolling left, you can see all Stories that the people you follow have published in the last 24 hours. The post vanishes 24 hours after it was posted.

Instagram always takes you to the content you haven't seen in that person's Story. For instance, if you watched two out of five Stories by someone, Instagram would play the third Story in the sequence when you came back within the 24-hour window of the post. Each person's Story has white dashes at the top that indicate the number of Stories for that person that day.

Here's how you navigate between Stories:

>> To skip an individual Story, tap on the right of the screen.

>> To skip an entire profile's Stories sequence, swipe left.

>> To see the previous Story, tap in the upper-left corner of the screen.

>> To pause a Story, tap and hold down on the screen.

Getting Started

Instagram Stories are a fun little add-on to Instagram and there are tons of features to explore! In this section, find out about the nuts and bolts of creating a basic Story either within the app or by taking and then uploading a photo or video. In the next chapter, you discover the more advanced features: text, stickers, hashtags, filters, and more.

Creating an Instagram Story in the app

Creating an Instagram Story in the app is simple: You can take photos or record a 15-second video. We go into more detail about adding stickers, hashtags, and filters in the next chapter.

To get started creating a photo or video Story, follow these steps:

1. **From your newsfeed (home screen), swipe right or tap the camera icon at the top left of the screen.**

   You can also tap your profile picture with the blue plus sign in the row of stories at the top of your screen.

   Make sure the setting at the bottom of the screen is Normal, as shown in Figure 9-2.

2. **Take a photo or a video:**

- *To take a photo, hold the phone up vertically and tap the white circle (refer to Figure 9-2).*

- *To take a video, hold down on the white circle.* A colorful bar outlines the circle to help you know when your 15 seconds (the maximum time) is up.

If you want the phone in selfie mode (camera facing you versus away from you), tap the two arrows located to the right of the white circle before you tap the white circle.

TIP

You can film a video that shows in reverse by using the Rewind setting. At the bottom of the screen, swipe left from the Normal setting until you see Rewind. Tap and hold down on the white button to record.

3. **To retake the photo or video, tap the X at the top left of the screen, and repeat Step 2.**

4. **To add a photo filter to your photo or video, swipe right on the photo until you reach the filter option you want.**

5. **If you'd like to save the photo or video, tap Save.**

You can then access it from your camera roll to email, text, or post on other social media.

You have another opportunity to save the photo or video later, after it posts, which we discuss in the "Saving Your Story" section of this chapter.

TIP

If you'd like to save all your Stories automatically every time, tap the gear icon (Settings) on the Stories screen, slide Save Shared Photos to the right, and then tap Done.

6. **Make the Story available:**

- *To make the Story available to all your followers, tap Your Story at the bottom of the screen.* It will post at the top of your followers' newsfeed.

FIGURE 9-2:
Tap or hold down on the white circle to take a photo or video, respectively.

- *To send the Story as a direct message (DM) that disappears after the person views it, tap Next. The screen shown in Figure 9-3 appears. Select the people to whom you want to send the DM, and then tap Send.*

  For details about sending DMs, skip to the section in this chapter titled "Using Direct Messages to Send a Story."

TIP

To film a video without the hassle of holding down the button the entire time, use the Hands-Free setting. Swiping left from the Normal setting until you reach Hands-Free. You can then record video by tapping the white circle with the colorful box inside. Filming will stop automatically after 15 seconds.

When you use the Boomerang setting, Instagram takes a burst of photos and stitches them together to create a mini video that then plays forward and backward — like a boomerang.

Uploading a photo or video from your camera roll

Sometimes, you may prefer to upload a photo or video stored on your camera roll instead of capturing it in the Instagram app.

TIP

In the past, Instagram Stories would load only photos or videos taken in the last 24 hours. Luckily, that has changed, and you can now access your entire camera roll. When you swipe up or tap the small photo icon to load a photo or video, you see photos from the last 24 hours first. If you keep scrolling up, you'll see your entire camera roll, and can load older items by tapping them.

Follow these steps to upload a photo or video to Instagram Stories:

1. **Swipe right from the newsfeed or tap the camera icon at the top of the newsfeed to access Instagram Stories.**

2. **Swipe up from the bottom of the screen or tap the box with a small photo thumbnail at the bottom left.**

   Thumbnails of all available photos and videos are displayed at the bottom of the screen, as shown in Figure 9-4.

3. **Tap the photo or video you'd like to post.**

4. **To add a photo filter to your photo or video, swipe right until you reach the filter option you want.**

5. **Tap Your Story to post your Story, or tap Next to send it as a direct message to an individual or group.**

   See Step 6 in the preceding section for details on direct messages.

FIGURE 9-4: Swipe up from the bottom of the Instagram Stories screen to see available photos to post.

Saving Your Story

Sometimes Stories are so good, you can't bear the thought of them disappearing forever. Well, you're in luck. You can save them to enjoy later and to repost on other social media networks in the following three ways:

>> **Save before you post your Story.** After you create or upload a photo or video, tap Save, located at the bottom left of the screen (see Figure 9-5). You must do this before you tap Your Story or Next.

>> **Save after you've posted your Story (within the 24-hour window).** Go to the newsfeed or your profile page and tap your profile picture. If you have an active Story, it will appear. Tap the right side of the screen until you see the Story you want to save. Tap the three small dots at the bottom right of the screen, and then tap Save (see Figure 9-6).

>> **Automatically save all your Stories to your camera roll.** Tap the gear icon (Settings) at the top left of the Stories page. On the Story Settings screen, slide Save Shared Photos to the right, and then tap Done.

FIGURE 9-5:
You can save your Story before you post it.

FIGURE 9-6:
You can save your story after you've posted it as well.

Using Direct Messages to Send a Story

Would you prefer to send a quick message to a client, prospective client, colleague, or group of people instead of posting in the general Stories area for your entire following to see? A direct message (DM) is the answer.

Follow these steps to send a Story via a direct message:

1. **Create your Story in the app or upload a photo or video.**

Directions for both are in the beginning of this section.

2. **Tap Next at the bottom right of your screen.**

The Send To screen appears.

3. **Select individuals to send the Story to by tapping the circle to the right of their username, as shown in Figure 9-7.**

You can still add the Story for all your followers to view by tapping Your Story on this new page instead of sending it via DM.

4. **Tap Send.**

Alternatively, you can create a group to and then send them a direct message with your Story:

1. **Create your Story in the app or upload a photo or video.**

2. **Tap Next.**

3. **Tap New Group, at the top of the Send To screen (refer to Figure 9-7).**

4. **(Optional) In the Name Group field, type a group name.**

   In Figure 9-8, Marketing Friends is a group name.

   If you type a group name, you can reuse the group later, which is handy if you send DMs to the same set of people often. The group name will be available to you in the Suggested area the next time you send a Story via DM.

5. **Tap the circle by the usernames you'd like to add to the group, as shown in Figure 9-8 (right).**

6. **Tap Create at the top of the screen to create the new group.**

   The group is then available for you, preselected on the next page.

7. **Tap Send.**

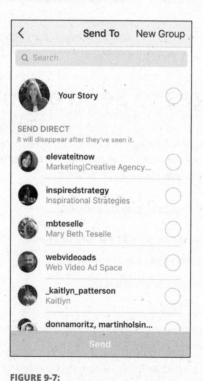

FIGURE 9-7:
Send a direct message to individuals.

FIGURE 9-8:
You can also send a direct message to a group.

Determining the Best Content to Share

Instagram Stories was designed to be a looser, less perfect area of Instagram. Many Instagrammers agonize over choosing the right photo or caption for their newsfeed so their aesthetic is maintained flawlessly. Instagram Stories allows those users to offer a less polished version of themselves or their business. In this section, we detail some of the common ways businesses use Instagram Stories to promote their brand, products, and services.

Talking to your audience

The popularity of video has surged in the last few years, so what better way to grab your audience's attention than talking to them via Instagram Stories? Talking directly to your audience gives them a familiarity with you and your business that can't be matched through still images. See Figure 9-9.

A problem with a Story video is that the maximum 15-second length means you have to combine videos for a longer conversation, which can result in a choppy video from all the stops and starts. The Storeo app (available as a free download in the iOS App Store) solves this issue. You upload one long video to its app, and it slices the video into the 15-second clips required by Instagram. The result is a Story video that flows more smoothly, with little disruption between each clip.

FIGURE 9-9:
@MartinHolsinger talks to his target audience of residential contractors through Instagram Stories videos.

Providing before-and-after and series shots

Stories are meant to be played in a series continuously, so before-and-after images or a series of photos work well to draw in followers. Using *before* and *after* labels or using small bits of text on a series can encourage followers to stick with your Story until the end.

Hairstylists, home decorators, stagers, remodelers, plastic surgeons, makeup artists, and landscapers have a great time creating before-and-after images in Instagram Stories, as you can see in Figure 9-10.

FIGURE 9-10: @egglestonde-signs uses before-and-after shots to show her home staging skills.

Products and services can also be showcased in a creative series that keeps follow-ers on a path to see what's next. See the example shown in Figure 9-11.

Whether using before-and-after photos or a series, add a graphic or video at the end, giving followers a call to action based on the information you've shared.

FIGURE 9-11: @glwheeler76 showcases her jewelry in a fun series with a call to action at the end.

Peeking behind the scenes

Because many Instagrammers are involved in launches, events, conferences, podcasts, and other exciting activities, behind-the-scenes Stories are a great way to let your audience in on how the magic really happens.

Whether it's showing the types of equipment used (see Figure 9-12), hanging decorations for an exclusive party, or interviewing speakers backstage before a conference starts, followers love to get to know more about how your business works through behind-the-scenes Stories.

Showing your travels

There's something so interesting about traveling to other places via Instagram Stories. You can watch someone sipping coffee in Vienna, and then in the next moment see another person at a convention in Minnesota.

Business people will often chronicle their travel to conferences or meetings, or showcase the luxury vacation they earned by working hard at their business all year, as shown in Figure 9-13.

© Brian Fanzo

FIGURE 9-12:
@isocialfanz shows his followers the equipment he uses to record his Instagram Stories.

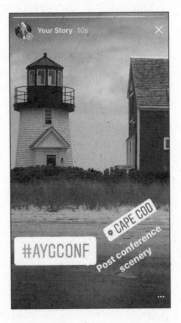

FIGURE 9-13:
@coreycwalker shows her followers her conference travel to Cape Cod.

Advertising Your Story

Although we always encourage engagement as a way to organically grow your following and new customers, sometimes it's not enough. Or maybe you're planning a promotion or an event that you want to tell your target audience right away. That's when advertising your Stories makes perfect sense.

You can run a campaign solely on Instagram Stories, or use it to complement a campaign you're running via the newsfeed. Just like an Instagram ad on the newsfeed, you can choose a target audience that is not following you already. For more information about the specs of an Instagram Stories ad and the available action links, see Chapter 11.

An Instagram Stories ad is labeled *Sponsored* at the top left and has an action link at the bottom of the page (Learn More in Figure 9-14). Users swipe up on the action link to go to the website you've chosen.

At this time, you can advertise on Instagram Stories only through Facebook Ads Manager, not through the Instagram mobile app. We detail exact steps for creating an Instagram Stories ad in Chapter 12.

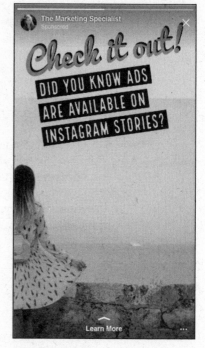

FIGURE 9-14:
Instagram Stories ads have a call to action at the bottom of the screen.

Chapter **10**

Making Your Story More Fun

n Chapter 9, we show you how to create and share a basic Instagram Story. There is so much more you can add to your Stories to make them come alive and get seen by more people!

Instagram Stories has rolled out a number of additions to enhance the Stories you create. In this chapter, we discuss how to create your own graphics; add text, username tags, stickers, hashtags, geolocation tags, and website links; and use Boomerang and face filters.

In addition, you find out how to use Instagram LIVE, including how to prepare for, promote, save, and repurpose your broadcast.

Creating Graphics for Stories

If you enjoy posting graphics versus photos, you'll be happy to hear that you can use graphics in Instagram Stories. Create your graphic in Illustrator or Photoshop, making sure the graphic is 1,080 pixels wide x 1,920 pixels high. Export the graphic as a .jpg, and email it to yourself.

Next, open the email on your phone, and download it to your camera roll. Then upload the graphic to Instagram Stories in the same way you upload a photo. (For details on uploading to Stories, see Chapter 9.)

If you don't have Illustrator or Photoshop, we recommend using Adobe Spark (https://spark.adobe.com/) to create your graphics. It's much simpler for someone without design experience to use. Adobe Spark is available on your phone (which saves the step of emailing the graphic) and includes Instagram Stories templates, which you can alter. You can also create your own design.

To create an Instagram Story graphic on your phone using Adobe Spark, follow these instructions:

1. **Download the Adobe Spark app from the App Store and create a username and password.**

   You can also log in through Facebook or Google. The app is free to use, but some photos and illustrations cost $1 each, and are clearly marked in the app.

2. **Choose a design:**

   - *Tap a category at the top of the screen, such as Lifestyle, Business, School, or Travel, as shown in Figure 10-1. Make a selection in the list of designs in that category that appear.*

   - *Tap a design in the Featured section.*

3. **Tap Remix.**

   The screen shown in Figure 10-2 appears.

4. **Change the design by tapping the options below the image:**

   - **Add:** Add text or a new photo by tapping on your choice. Then either type new text and tap Done, or select photo library to access your photos, access the camera roll to take a photo, or search free photos to use a stock photo. Tap the photo you would like to use and it will be added to your design.

   - **Design:** Change the look and feel of your post by tapping Design, and then choosing one of the other suggested designs. Your photo or background will remain the same, but the font and filter will change. Tap Done after you find a design you like. Premium paid customers can also add their own fonts and filters in the Brand section, and add those to a design.

   - **Palette:** In the Palette section, you can change the color scheme of your image and text. Several color palettes are available. To change the color palette, simply tap a new palette. Tap Done to save the palette to your design.

FIGURE 10-1:
Adobe Spark offers categories and featured designs that you can alter.

FIGURE 10-2:
Customize a template design's photo, layout, and more.

- **Resize:** Resize your design according to its use. You can choose correct sizing for a Facebook ad, Instagram, Instagram Stories, YouTube, and more. Tap the size you want, and then tap Done.

- **Layout:** Alter the layout of your image by changing the grid. (This change will typically prompt you to upload more photos, depending on the layout you select.) Tap the grid you like, and then tap Done. To add more photos, tap Add and following the instructions detailed earlier in this section about adding photos.

- **Effects:** Change filters by selecting one of the filters at the bottom of the screen, or choose Animation and select how you would like to animate your images. After you select a filter or an animation, tap Done.

5. **When you're satisfied with your graphic, tap Share. Then choose Save Post as either Video or Image (no animation) to save the graphic to your camera roll.**

WARNING

On the next screen, do not tap the Instagram icon. Selecting that will send the graphic to your main Instagram newsfeed, not to Instagram Stories.

6. **Upload the graphic just as you would upload a photo to Instagram Stories.**

   For details on uploading a photo to Stories, see Chapter 9.

TIP

When you create an image in Adobe Spark, it saves the image in My Posts. For future images, it may be easier to use My Posts to alter one of your own designs if you normally stick to similar colors, styles, and fonts for your brand. The editing features and sharing process are the same as using one of Adobe Spark's templates.

Canva (www.canva.com) is another popular app that allows you to create graphics based on its templates. However, it doesn't have a template sized exactly for Instagram Stories.

Adding Text and Username Tags

Adding text to your photo or video can add context (and often humor) to your Story. You can also tag another user using text. Follow these steps to add text or username tags:

1. **Take a photo or video in Instagram Stories, or upload a photo or video there.**

2. **Tap Aa at the top right of your screen, as shown in Figure 10-3, left.**

   A new screen with a keyboard appears.

3. **Type your word or phrase (emojis work here too), as shown in Figure 10-3, right.**

   You can change the text color and size:

   • *To change the text color from white, the default, tap a colored circle. Scroll left or right to reveal more color choices or tap and hold down on a color circle to reveal another color selection palette.*

   • *To change the type size, find the slider on the left side of the page and move it up or down.*

4. **If you want to tag someone, type @username and select the person from the suggested profiles.**

   The person will be notified that you tagged him or her in your Story.

5. **Tap Done.**

Stickers   Text

Draw   Text color   Block text

FIGURE 10-3:
To add text, tap
Aa in the
top-right of the
screen (left) and
then use the
keyboard (right).

New journals!

6. **(Optional) Make further changes:**

   • *Move the text by tapping and holding down on the text and then sliding it to its new position.*

   • *Change the type size by placing two fingers on the text and sliding your fingers apart or together.*

   • *Change the angle of the text by placing two fingers on the text and twisting left or right.*

7. **Share the Story by tapping Your Story; save it by tapping Save; or send it as a DM by tapping Next, selecting the recipients, and tapping Send.**

TIP

To create block text (white text that has a color boxed behind it), tap the A at the top of the keyboard screen (labeled in Figure 10-3, right). Tapping the A again makes the background transparent, and tapping again removes the transparency.

Drawing on Your Story

Another popular feature of Instagram Stories is the drawing tool. You can use your finger to draw arrows, to circle something, to write words, or to draw anything else you'd like!

Follow these steps to draw on a Story:

1. **Take a photo or video in Instagram Stories, or upload a photo or video there.**

2. **Tap the pen icon at the top right of the screen (refer to Figure 10-3, left).**

3. **Tap a drawing tool, at the top of the screen.**

From left to right, the tools are as follows:

- *Magic marker:* Draws like a fat magic marker.

- *Highlighter:* Draws like a highlighter and is slightly transparent.

- *Neon:* Draws like a neon light with an outline of the color you select.

- *Eraser:* Erases anything you draw. Use your finger to rub across the drawing to erase. Erasing will not affect your photo or video.

- *Heart:* Draws like a piece of chalk.

4. **Start drawing! You can use your finger or a stylus.**

See what each drawing tool's line looks like in Figure 10-4. You can change the color or line width as follows:

- *To change the color of any drawing tool (except the eraser), tap a colored circle (at the bottom of the screen).*

- *To change the line width, tap the circle to the left of the other colored circles, and move the slider up or down.*

5. **When you have finished drawing, tap Done at the top right of the screen.**

You can still go back and erase or add to your drawing by tapping the pen tool again.

FIGURE 10-4:
You can draw with a magic marker, highlighter, neon, and chalk.

6. **Share the Story by tapping Your Story; save it by tapping Save; or send it as a DM by tapping Next, selecting the recipients, and tapping Send.**

TIP

When you have text that is hard to read over a busy photo or video, make the text stand out by scribbling behind it. Or, if you'd like to create a solid color background that covers the entire screen, take a photo of anything, tap the drawing tool, select a color, and then tap and hold down anywhere on the screen.

Stickers and Tags

The sticker page is available after you take or upload a photo or video. Simply tap the square smiley face at the top of the screen (refer to Figure 10-3). Stickers are an easy way to add color and fun to your photos or videos. Instagram changes its stickers based on the day or holiday. For instance, on Sundays, you'll see SundayFunday stickers, as shown in Figure 10-5. Leading up to Halloween, you'll see pumpkins, witches, and goblins.

The sticker page is also where you can find location geotags, the temperature and time for your location, hashtags, and photo stickers.

To add a sticker, simply follow these steps:

1. **Take a photo or video in Instagram Stories, or upload a photo or video there.**

2. **Tap the icon for stickers (labeled in 10-3, left.)**

FIGURE 10-5:
You can choose from a variety of stickers.

A screen with stickers appears. Three screens are available, as indicated by the dots near the top of the screen. Tap the left dot to access recently used stickers. The middle dot displays the main screen with the latest and most popular stickers, as well as geotags, hashtags, selfie photos, temperature, and time. The right dot displays a page of stickers of hats and glasses. Swipe up on any sticker page to see more.

3. **Tap the sticker you want to add.**

- *If you tapped the Location sticker: Tap one of the locations that are presented to you.*

   That location is added as a geotag to your Story, and your Story is added to all other Stories currently using that geotag. This is a great way to get your Story seen by local people who don't necessarily follow you. See Figure 10-6 (left).

- *If you tapped the #Hashtag sticker: Type your hashtag using the keyboard that appears. Then tap Done.*

   As you type, Instagram offers suggestions for your tag; you can select one if you want. Your Story is added to all other Stories currently using that hashtag. Now anyone who searches that hashtag can see your Story. See Figure 10-6 (middle).

- *If you tapped the camera icon: Tap and hold down on the gray blob that appears, and then move it to the desired location. Hold your phone up to your face; your face appears inside the gray blob. If you want a white circle around your face, tap the gray blob. When ready, tap the white circle below the gray blob or the large white circle to add a selfie photo sticker to your photo or video. See 10-6 (right).*

FIGURE 10-6: You can add your location (left), a hashtag (middle), or a selfie photo (right) to your Story.

4. **Adjust the position, size, or angle of the sticker as desired:**

   - *Move the sticker by tapping and holding down on the sticker and then sliding it.*

   - *Change the size by placing two fingers on the sticker and then sliding your fingers apart or together.*

   - *Change the angle of the sticker by placing two fingers on the sticker and then twisting left or right.*

5. **Share the Story by tapping Your Story; save it by tapping Save; or send it as a DM by tapping Next, selecting the recipients, and tapping Send.**

Adding a Link to Your Website

A popular feature that is available only to business profiles with 10,000 or more followers is adding a link to your website. This is an important addition because it offers a direct way for businesses to send people to their website to get more information, register for events, or make a purchase. To add a website link:

1. **Take a photo or video in Instagram Stories, or upload a photo or video there.**

2. **Tap the chain link icon (see Figure 10-7, left) at the top of your Story.**

   A new page appears.

3. **Type your website destination (see Figure 10-7, right.)**

4. **Tap Done (iOS) or the green check mark (Android).**

Your followers will see a *See More* link at the bottom of your Story, indicating a website link. Make sure you add a call to action either verbally during your video or by adding *Swipe Up to See More* overlay text to a still image.

TIP

Instagram doesn't track links on Stories. To capture the analytics on your website clicks, use a URL shortener such as Bitly (`https://bitly.com`) or Rebrandly (`www.rebrandly.com`), and then access metrics via its dashboard.

FIGURE 10-7:
A chain link at the
top of your Story
means you can
add a link (left).
Add your website
destination link
on the next
page (right).

Using Boomerang to Keep Fans Coming Back

Boomerang is an app that takes a burst of photos and creates a looping backward and forward video clip from them. An action such as twirling a pencil or blowing a bubble becomes more exciting when played in a loop!

Boomerang is not installed automatically on your phone. Go to the App Store and type **Boomerang for Instagram** in the Search bar to find it (it's free). After you download the app, follow these steps to use it:

1. **Open Instagram Stories by swiping right or using the camera icon at the top of the newsfeed.**

2. **Slide the Normal setting to the left, changing it to Boomerang, as shown in Figure 10-8.**

3. **To switch from forward-facing video mode to selfie video mode and back, tap the arrows to the right of the white circle (and shown in the margin).**

   You can also use Boomerang with one of the face filters, as described in the next section.

4. **Tap the white circle with the Boomerang logo (infinity symbol).**

   You don't need to hold down the white button as you would for video. The app is actually taking several pictures in a rapid burst.

5. **If you're not satisfied with your Boomerang and want to try again, tap X at the top left and repeat, starting Step 3.**

6. **Share the Boomerang Story by tapping Your Story; save it by tapping Save; or send it as a DM by tapping Next, selecting the recipients, and tapping Send.**

FIGURE 10-8:
Boomerang is to the right of the Normal setting.

TIP

Boomerang works best when recording movement. To try it out, film someone doing a cartwheel, making funny faces in the camera, or dancing!

Making Funny Faces with Face Filters

A face filter is an app that applies a filter over your face using the camera, making you look, for example, like a dog, an alien, or a rock star. Instagram Stories didn't offer face filters when it first launched, so a lot of people continued using Snapchat for that feature, or created Snaps with filters and then loaded them to Instagram Stories. Now, Instagram users can rejoice at the fact that their favorite feature of Snapchat is available on Instagram!

Here's how it works:

1. **Open Instagram Stories by swiping right or using the camera icon at the top of the newsfeed.**

2. **Put the camera in selfie mode by tapping the arrows to the right of the white circle (and shown in the margin).**

3. **Tap the smiling face to the right of the selfie mode arrows.**

   Filters appear at the bottom of the screen. Scroll to the left to see all available filters.

4. **To apply a filter to your face, as shown in Figure 10-9, tap the filter.**

   To change filters, simply tap a different one.

5. **Take a photo by tapping the white button, or record a video by holding down the white button.**

   You can use filters in any camera setting: Live, Boomerang, Rewind, or Hands-Free.

6. **To try again, tap the X at the top left of the page and go back to Step 4.**

7. **Share your Story by tapping Your Story; save it by tapping Save; or send it as a DM by tapping Next, selecting the recipients, and tapping Send.**

FIGURE 10-9:
Instagram Stories offer fun face filters that alter your appearance to look like an animal, a character, and so much more.

REMEMBER

Using Instagram LIVE

Quickly after it launched, Instagram Stories dramatically changed the way people used Instagram. Some users even abandoned the newsfeed and went all in on Instagram Stories. With the popularity of Stories and the growth of Facebook LIVE, including a live video option in Instagram Stories seemed like a natural next step.

In this section, you learn all about how to go live, and get tips for making your LIVE broadcast more successful before, during, and after filming.

Getting started with LIVE

So, you're ready to go LIVE, but how do you even get to it? Its location is not exactly obvious. Follow these steps:

1. **Open Instagram Stories by swiping right or using the camera icon at the top of the newsfeed.**

2. **At the bottom of the screen, swipe Normal to the right so you are on LIVE.**

   Figure 10-10, left, shows the LIVE screen.

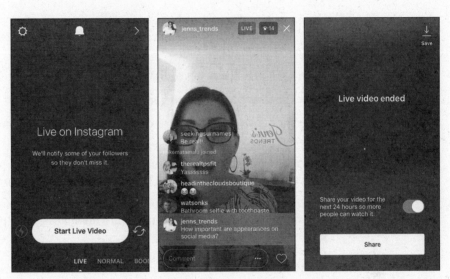

FIGURE 10-10: Before going LIVE (left), going LIVE (middle), and saving your broadcast (right).

3. **If you want only certain people to view your LIVE broadcast, tap the gear icon (Settings) at the top left. Tap Hide Story From, and select the followers you want to omit.**

   You can also turn off notifications by tapping the bell icon at the top of the screen. However, we recommend leaving notifications on so your followers can be alerted that you're starting.

4. **When you're ready to start, tap Start Live Video.**

   Instagram checks your connection, and then the timer counts down 3, 2, 1 and you're on! You'll begin seeing "*Username* has joined" and the number of people who have joined.

5. **Wait a minute or two before diving into your topic so that people have time to join. Greet as many people as possible.**

6. **Now that you're LIVE, you can do the following:**

- *Turn off comments by tapping the three dots at the bottom right of the screen, as shown in Figure 10-10, middle.* However, we recommend that you keep them turned on for more interaction.

- *Enter the name of your LIVE broadcast by typing it in a comment and tapping Send. Then tap the comment and choose Pin Comment from the options menu.* This pins the name to the top of the comment feed, where it acts like a title.

- *To keep track of your time, tap the pink LIVE button in the upper right.* A timer appears.

- *To see the names of the people who have joined, tap the number to the right of the pink LIVE button. To kick people out of your LIVE broadcast, place an X by their name.*

7. **When you're finished, tap End, and then tap End Live Video.**

8. **Save the LIVE video by tapping Save at the top left.**

   Your video is saved to your camera roll so you can use it elsewhere online, as shown in Figure 10-10, right.

   WARNING

   You must save your LIVE broadcast immediately after recording (before you agree to share it). After it's shared, there is no option to go back and save it.

9. **To share the LIVE video with your Instagram followers for 24 hours, go to the bottom of your screen and make sure the sharing tab is pushed to the right showing blue, then tap Share.**

WARNING

Instagram LIVE has a 60-minute time limit. You'll see a 15-second timer countdown when your time is almost up, and then the LIVE broadcast will shut down at the 60-minute mark. Plan your content accordingly!

Developing a game plan

Now that you know how to physically tap all the buttons to record a LIVE broadcast, it's time to talk strategy. We recommend going on Instagram LIVE with forethought about what you'll be doing. Here are a few tips to help you execute the best Instagram LIVE possible:

>> **Think of a topic that will interest your audience.** Some ideas to consider: Announce a new product, discuss industry news, teach a class, or offer a Q&A session.

>> **Jot down several talking points, but don't memorize or look overly rehearsed.** LIVE broadcasts are supposed to be a bit off the cuff.

- » **Think about some common questions you might get asked, and prepare your answers.** You can also ask people to submit questions beforehand.

- » **Do a test video on your regular camera app where you plan to do the LIVE broadcast, and at the same time of day.** Check the lighting and the background. Make sure that you can get a decent signal in that location.

- » **Promote your LIVE broadcast ahead of time via Instagram, your blog, your email list, and other social networks.**

- » **Be as interactive as possible with your followers during the broadcast.**

- » **Save your broadcast so you can repurpose it to other online media, and then publish your broadcast so it's available for 24 hours.**

TIP

It's often helpful to have a tripod to hold your camera steady and in place while filming LIVE. Arkon Mounts (www.arkon.com/) has several tripods available for under $50.

Alerting your fans

To help get more viewers to your LIVE video, promote it. You can do this in a variety of ways, but the most obvious route is through Instagram itself. Post a graphic or a video in your Instagram newsfeed and Stories stating the topic, date, and time, as shown in Figure 10-11. If you have an email newsletter or blog, you'll want to promote it there too. Finally, reach out to your other social media networks, and post information about the LIVE video there, making sure to include your Instagram handle.

Instagram sends a notification to your followers (unless they have turned off this feature) to let them know you are LIVE. Your profile pic will be labeled *LIVE* in the bar at the top of the newsfeed so people can jump in from there too.

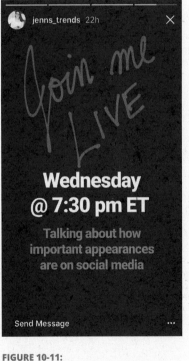

FIGURE 10-11:
Post graphics on Instagram before your LIVE broadcast to promote it.

Acknowledging LIVE followers

While you're waiting for more people to view your LIVE video, acknowledge with excitement the people who are joining you. Use their name and thank them for participating. After a few minutes, you can start speaking about the topic.

People will likely comment while you're talking. It's nice to answer questions and comments as they arise, but sometimes it's not practical if you're trying to explain something. In this case, let them know that you are happy to take comments and questions, and will address them at the end.

Saving and repurposing LIVE broadcasts

After you've completed your LIVE broadcast, don't forget to save it! After you've tapped End Live Video, tap Save in the screen that appears (refer to Figure 10-10, right). The broadcast is saved to your camera.

When you save your Instagram LIVE broadcast, it becomes a regular video that you can use any way you'd like. Here are some places to reuse it:

>> On your website

>> In a blog post

>> In your email newsletter as a free replay, or as a teaser for your next LIVE broadcast

>> On your YouTube channel, then share the link to it on LinkedIn and Twitter

>> On your Facebook business page

You can also edit the video to create 1-minute or less sound bites, and upload them directly to Instagram, Facebook, LinkedIn, and Twitter. Or create a graphic about the video for Instagram, and then link to the video (on YouTube or your website) via the link in the bio on your Instagram profile page.

You can reuse LIVE content in so many creative ways — don't let it go to waste!

Chapter **11**

Planning a Winning Ad

With over 700 million people using Instagram each month and 80 percent of those following a business on Instagram, advertising on Instagram is a no-brainer. The demographics are shifting older too — Instagram is no longer just a playground for teens and Gen Y. If you're seeking Gen X or even some Baby Boomers customers, Instagram is quickly becoming a hotspot for them too.

In this chapter, we discuss choosing an ad type, the design elements needed for a good Instagram post, and selecting your target audience, which may include those Baby Boomers!

REMEMBER

You must have your Instagram account set up as a business profile to create ads. For more information about this easy (and free) upgrade, refer to Chapter 2.

Selecting the Right Ad Type

Four types of Instagram ads are available:

» **Photo:** A stunning simple square or landscape photo with a call to action link.

» **Video:** Up to one minute of square or landscape video, including sound and call to action link.

>> **Carousel:** Two to ten photos or videos or both that users can swipe through to get in-depth information. Includes one call to action link for the entire sequence.

>> **Stories:** Photos or videos in this newer section of Instagram to complement other content in your regular feed.

INSTAGRAM DEMOGRAPHICS

Pew Research Center conducted a social media report in November 2016 that outlined key usage demographics. Usage by age range follows:

- 18-29 years: 59%

- 30-39 years: 33%

- 50-64 years: 18%

- 65+ years: 8%

As you can see, Instagram is still a strong platform for younger audiences, but the numbers for older adults (with more money to spend) are increasing rapidly. Women are more prevalent users on Instagram than men: 38 percent of women use Instagram, while only 26 percent of men use it. Users are slightly higher in the cities (39 percent), but that is changing too, with 31 percent of adults living in rural areas and 28 percent of adults living in suburban areas using Instagram.

The reasons for using Instagram for your advertising platform are even better:

- Demographics are highly targetable via Facebook's extensive shared database.

- The cost of entry is low. You can run a successful ad campaign for less than $20 if you use the right creative and targeting strategy!

- You can reach a new set of customers who haven't discovered your profile yet.

- It's the perfect tool to drive traffic to your website, opt-in piece, or other link of your choice.

Ads can be used separately or blended together to create a well-rounded campaign that delights different audience preferences. A huge advantage of Instagram ads is that they allow call-to-action links directly below the image.

All ads display *Sponsored* in the top-right corner of the image to let users know that they are seeing a paid ad.

Normally, the only link available to you on Instagram is in the bio on your profile page. Having a call-to-action link below the image is a big deal!

Photo ad

A *photo ad*, like the one in Figure 11-1, is the simplest ad type, using only one photo or image in square or landscape format. Photo (and video) ads offer two objectives to choose from when you create them in the Instagram app. You can choose Get More Profile and Website Views or Reach People Near an Address. Depending on which objective you choose, different call-to-action links are available.

For the Get More Profile and Website Views objective, your call-to-action link choices are as follows:

>> Book Now

>> Contact Us

>> Learn More

>> Shop Now

>> Sign Up

>> Watch More

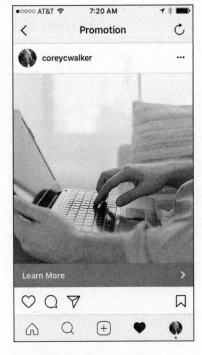

FIGURE 11-1:
This photo ad has a Learn More call-to-action link that links to the company's website.

Each option allows you to link to a website or your Instagram business profile.

The Reach People Near an Address objective provides the following call-to-action link choices:

>> Get Directions

>> Call Now

Get Directions enables you to enter an address and offers step-by-step directions from the user's location to the address you entered. Call Now allows you to enter a phone number, and provides a link to call when tapped.

If you use Facebook Ads Manager to create your Instagram photo (or video) ad, many more objectives are available: brand awareness, reach, traffic, app installs, engagement, conversions, video views, product catalog sales, store visits, and lead generation. Depending on the objective of your ad, you may need to use Ads Manager for a more targeted approach.

We walk through creating the ad in Instagram's mobile app and Facebook in the next chapter.

Video ad

A *video ad* enables you to boost your message with the power of a one-minute video. Video is becoming more popular and mainstream. It can capture your audience's attention in a stronger way than a still photo can. Tell a quick story, show how to use your product, ask your audience a question — you can engage with your audience in so many ways through video.

Video ads provide the same objectives and call-to-action links described in the preceding section, "Photo ads." Figure 11-2 shows an example of a video ad with a Sign Up call-to-action link. If recording video is new to you, refer to Chapter 5 to learn how to film, edit, and post videos on Instagram.

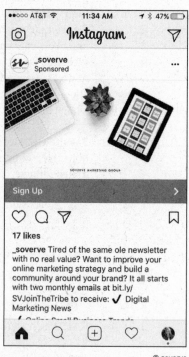

© soverve

FIGURE 11-2:
This video ad has a Sign Up call-to-action link that links to the company's website.

Carousel ad

You use a carousel ad to tell a visual story with two to ten still images or videos or both. Instead of relying on one image or video, the carousel allows your audience to be walked through an event, with step-by-step instructions, demonstrations of your product, before-and-after presentations, or even one long, scrolling panoramic image.

When you create a carousel ad, you can select the order in which the images or videos are shown. If you don't need them to follow a particular order, you can tell Instagram to arrange them to show the highest performing image or video first.

TIP

Always choose an engaging image or video as your first piece of content in a carousel. Users likely won't bother scrolling through the carousel if the main image in the feed doesn't appeal to them.

A carousel ad is square and allows only one caption and comment feed for the entire sequence (not separate captions and comments for each photo). In the newsfeed, users briefly see a black oval with 1/# (where # is the number of images or videos in the carousel) in the top right of your carousel. They also see blue dots at the bottom of the image that represent the number of images or videos in the carousel, as shown in Figure 11-3. This way, they know to scroll left to see the entire carousel.

You can't create a carousel ad in the Instagram mobile app. This type of ad is available only in Facebook Ad Manager and Power Editor.

The ad objectives for carousel ads are brand awareness, reach, traffic, app installs, engagement, conversions, video views, product catalog sales, store visits, and lead generation.

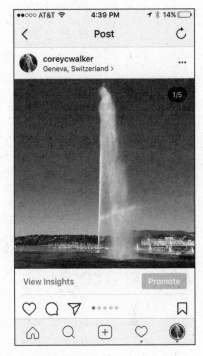

FIGURE 11-3:
The *1/5* in the top-right corner of the image and the five dots below the image tell you that this carousel ad has five images or videos.

Stories ad

The newest Instagram ad feature — and one that is gaining in popularity — is the ability to run ads through Instagram Stories. The easiest way to create a Stories ad is by using Facebook's Ad Manager, but you can also create them with Facebook's Power Editor. Unfortunately, there is no way to create a Stories ad with the Instagram mobile app.

You can use photos or videos in a Stories ad, but they must be in vertical format (versus the more common square in the newsfeed), with a suggested size of 1,080 x 1,920 pixels. This size offers the best resolution and fit to the screen. (However, if necessary, Instagram will resize your image to fit the screen.) Other dimensions may stretch or cut off parts of your photo or video.

Stories ads offer a large variety of call-to-action links:

>> Get Showtimes

>> Book Now

>> Download

>> Learn More

>> Shop Now

>> Send Message

>> Sign Up

>> Watch More

When users swipe up on the call-to-action link, they go to a website you chose when setting up the ad. Figure 11-4 shows an example of a Stories ad with a Learn More call to action.

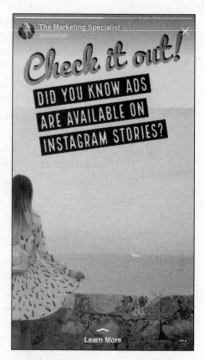

FIGURE 11-4:
Instagram Stories ads have a call to action at the bottom of the screen.

Using an Effective Ad Strategy

Now that you have learned about the different ad types available, it's time to get down to the nitty-gritty of designing the ad, from size specs to audience types and more.

Design requirements

The design requirements vary for each ad type we discussed previously in the chapter. In this section, we outline all the specs you need to create an ad in the correct size.

For photo, video, and carousel ads, use the following specs:

>> Image ratio: 1:1 (square), 1.91:1 (landscape), 4:5 (vertical). Carousel ads accommodate only square images and videos.

>> Image size minimum: 600 x 600 pixels (square), 600 x 315 pixels (landscape), 600 x 750 pixels (vertical).

>> Image size maximum: 1,936 x 1,936 pixels (all shapes).

>> Caption text: 125 characters recommended, up to 300 characters.

>> Video length: 60 seconds.

>> File type: .png or .jpg for photos, and .mp4 or .mov for videos.

>> File size max: 30MB for photos, 4GB for videos.

Some of the specs for Instagram Stories ads are different:

>> Image ratio: 4:5 (vertical only) or 9:16 for photos

>> Image size minimum: 600 x 1,067

>> Image size maximum: 1,080 x 1,920 pixels

>> Video length: 15 seconds

>> File type: .png or .jpg for photos, .mp4 or .mov for videos

>> File size max: 30MB for photos, 4GB for videos

Selecting your target audience

A wide variety of options are available to target your perfect audience. You have basic choices such as location and age, but you can also get specific and use people's interests, page likes, income levels, and more. Here are some of the many options available to you:

>> Location

>> Gender

>> Age range

>> Languages

>> Interests (health, guinea pigs, video games, floral design, specific Facebook pages, like Trader Joe's or 24 Hour Fitness, you name it)

>> Employers

>> Income level

>> Homeowner or renter

>> Single, married, divorced, widowed, in a relationship

>> Children or no children

» Connections (whether they are fans of your page, use your app, and so forth)

» Custom audiences (advanced feature that looks at people you already know using information you provide to Facebook to build a targeted audience)

» Lookalike audiences (subset of a custom audience that creates a new targeted audience that is similar to your existing custom audience)

Jot down a wider target audience using your ideal location, gender, and age first, and then write ideas for a narrower audience using more specific interests and demographics.

When building the ad in Facebook's Ads Manager or Power Editor, you can see whether your selections are too broad or specific by checking a meter that changes as you add or subtract characteristics. It will also give you an estimated daily reach based on your targeting selections and your budget, as shown in Figure 11-5.

If you find the audience is too broad, try adding a specific interest. If your audience is too narrow, there may not be enough people to see the ad. In this case, eliminate interests that are extremely niche to help your ad's daily reach.

Chapter 12 details how to create the audience in Facebook Ads Manager or Power Editor.

Audience Size

Your audience is defined.

Specific   Broad

Potential Reach: 1,100,000 people

Estimated Daily Results

Reach
4,500 - 17,000 (of 850,000)

Link Clicks
37 - 200 (of 9,200)

The accuracy of estimates is based on factors like past campaign data, the budget you entered and market data. Numbers are provided to give you an idea of performance for your budget, but are only estimates and don't guarantee results.

Were these estimates helpful?

FIGURE 11-5:
The meter displays the ad's estimated daily reach based on the demographics, interests, and budget you select.

Choosing ad images wisely

If you've been cruising around on Instagram for a while, you've surely noticed accounts that are simply amazing. The best accounts normally stick to a theme, use consistent colors or filters, and style their images in a certain way to create a unique brand look.

After you have your page's brand determined, it's important to choose an image for your ad that best represents your overall look. It should be obvious that the ad belongs with the rest of your images (or videos). In this section, we go over several ways to choose the best images for your ad.

Your ad will likely go to people who have never seen your profile page before. Choose a strong image that draws people into your account so they want to keep seeing more.

Use people

Using people in your ad helps to make a connection with your audience. Studies have found that candid photos versus perfectly staged photos perform better. And photos where the person is not looking at the camera, like the photo in Figure 11-6, perform the best. The theory is that it's easier for your audience to imagine themselves as that person if they are not posing for the camera.

Choose a pop of color

Your image should look like it belongs with the rest of your profile, but you also want your image to stand out and stop the scroll. A great way to achieve this is by incorporating a pop of bright color, as shown in Figure 11-7. The eye can't help but get drawn toward a bright image and stop at least briefly to find out what it is.

Create a mood

Creating a mood with your photo helps your audience picture themselves in the situation. Images that convey trust, security, and coziness tend to work best. (See Figure 11-8.) If these terms don't fit with your brand, choose a word that does, and try to find an image that expresses that feeling.

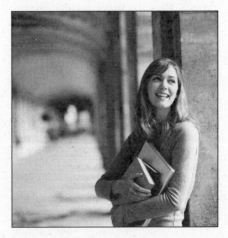

FIGURE 11-6:
Using people in your ad helps to forge a connection with your audience.

FIGURE 11-7:
A pop of bright color will get your ad noticed.

Lighting

There is nothing worse than a photo that is too dark, has weird shadows, or is washed out, as shown in Figure 11-9. Luckily, even photos that weren't taken in the best circumstances can often be fixed — and you don't have to be a Photoshop expert! For more in-depth coverage of great editing tools, refer to Chapter 4. If you can't get the image to look just right, choose an image with better lighting for your ad, and save that image for your regular feed.

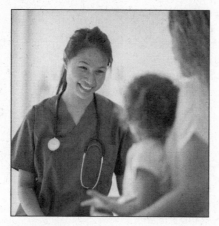

FIGURE 11-8:
The smile of this doctor conveys warmth and trust.

FIGURE 11-9:
Photos with bad lighting should never be used as an ad.

Clarity

There is actually something worse than bad lighting — photos that are blurry or grainy are the worst. Unlike bad lighting, it's almost impossible to fix a blurry or grainy photo. Your images should be at least 72 dpi for online use. Choosing a low quality image for an ad sets a bad impression right from the start. It leaves your audience wondering what other details might get overlooked if they work with you or buy your product. See Figure 11-10.

FIGURE 11-10:
Blurry or grainy photos are almost impossible to fix. Never use them in an ad.

TIP

If you have the time and resources to do a photo shoot, creating a custom image that fits your brand is best. If that isn't possible, check out stock photo companies such as iStock (`www.istockphoto.com`) or Adobe Stock (`https://stock.adobe.com`), which offer affordable royalty-free images at a reasonable rate.

A caption can speak (less than) 1,000 words

Although you can usually squeeze in 2,200 characters in a normal Instagram caption, Instagram ads require that you keep your captions short and sweet with a 300-character limit. Because only the first two to three lines are shown — people have to click the More link to see the rest — it's best to put your most important message at the beginning.

Here are some other tips to create a winning ad caption:

>> **Don't go in for the sale right away.** This audience is likely new to you. Let them get to know you by offering something of value to them for free, such as a checklist, email program, or sample product.

>> **Ask questions.** Create more engagement by asking your audience a question, and they will feel more inclined to comment.

>> **Tell them to tag a friend.** Another good engagement tip is to tell people to "Tag a friend who might like to see this, win this, wear this, and so on." When paired with an great image, your target audience will start sharing away!

>> **Provide details.** If the image doesn't instantly explain what your product or service is, use the caption to create deeper context with the image.

>> **Use only a few hashtags.** Although up to 30 hashtags in a comment below the initial caption are often used for a regular post, your ad doesn't work that way. Choose 1 to 3 hashtags that get to the heart of your message and place them in the caption. This is a great time to use a specialty hashtag created just for your brand.

>> **Include a call to action.** Last, but certainly not least, always include a call to action (CTA). This is the number-one thing you want people to do when they see your ad. Phrases such as *Tap the Learn More button for a free download* or *Sign up this week for our bonus offer* tell your audience exactly what they should do next to continue a relationship with you. Don't forget this crucial piece of the puzzle!

Chapter **12**

Creating an Effective Instagram Ad

After you decide what type of ad will work best for you, it's time to find out how to create the ad. In this chapter, we walk through the various ways you can create an Instagram ad, including creating it directly through Instagram's mobile app and two options from Facebook (Ads Manager and Power Editor). If you're planning on running the same creative campaign on Facebook, it's helpful to understand Facebook Ads Manager or Power Editor so your Instagram and Facebook campaigns are synced.

Facebook optimizes campaigns run on both platforms. Whichever platform is performing better (based on the objective you set) will get more ads shown.

TIP

We also cover the important topics of testing your ads and measuring the results. By making simple tweaks based on the data uncovered through testing and measuring, you can make a huge difference in the effectiveness of ongoing and new campaigns.

Using the Instagram Mobile App to Create an Ad

Photo ads and video ads can be created by using the Instagram mobile app. Carousel and Stories ads must be created by using Facebook Ads Manager, Facebook Power Editor, or Instagram's API (an area that developers use and that is beyond the scope of this book).

Here are the steps for creating a photo or video ad by using the Instagram mobile app:

1. **Post your photo or video with a caption, hashtags, and a location to Instagram as you normally would for a general post.**

2. **Click the blue Promote button, as shown in Figure 12-1.**

   A pop-up appears, asking whether you want to *Choose what you want this promotion to do.*

3. **To follow along with this example, choose Get More Profile and Website Visits.**

   The Create Promotion page shown in Figure 12-2 appears.

FIGURE 12-1:
Click the blue Promote button to start the ad process.

FIGURE 12-2:
The Create Promotion page offers several options.

4. **Tailor your campaign.**

- *Objective:* This field displays the option you just chose, either Get More Profile and Website Visits or Reach People Near an Address. You can change the objective by tapping the Objective field and choosing the other available option.

- *Destination:* This field displays the website currently linked to your Instagram profile page. To change this to another website or to your Instagram profile page, tap the Destination field and type the new website address or tap the other available destination. Your chosen destination will sport a blue arrow.

- *Action Button:* Choose a link phrase by tapping the Action Button field to display a list of call-to-action link phrases. Select a link phrase, and then tap Done.

- *Audience:* This field displays *Automatic* when Instagram chooses an audience for you. To create your own audience (which we recommend), tap the Audience field and then tap Create Your Own. On the next page, New Audience, name your audience, choose a location, interests, and age ranges, and decide whether you want to target men, women, or both. Then tap Done.

- *Budget:* Choose a budget by tapping the Budget field and selecting a total budget for your entire campaign. You can select an amount suggested by Instagram, or tap Set Your Own to choose a different amount. Instagram informs you how your budget breaks down into a daily budget based on the Duration (up next). After you've selected a budget, tap Done.

- *Duration:* Change the duration of your campaign by tapping the Duration field and selecting a suggested duration or by tapping the Set Your Own field and selecting a different duration. Then tap Done.

5. **After you have selected all your choices on the Create Promotion page, click Create Promotion.**

That's it — pretty easy, right?

Using Facebook to Create an Ad

Facebook offers two ways to create Instagram ads: Ads Manager and Power Editor. Facebook Ads Manager, which is the default, is easier to use than Power Editor. If you're unfamiliar with Facebook ads, we suggest that you start by using Ads Manager.

REMEMBER

You must have a Facebook business page and an ad account to run ads on Instagram.

Creating a photo, video, or carousel ad in Ads Manager

To create a photo, video, or carousel Instagram ad by using Ads Manager, follow these steps:

1. **Go to your Facebook business page. Click the small triangle at the top right of the screen and choose Create Ads from the drop-down menu. You can also type** www.facebook.com/ads/manager.

    The Ads Manager page appears, as shown in Figure 12-3.

2. **Choose your objective for the campaign and enter your campaign name.**

Campaign: Choose your objective.		Help: Choosing an Objective Use Existing Campaign
Awareness	**Consideration**	**Conversion**
Brand awareness	Traffic	Conversions
Reach	Engagement	Product catalog sales
	App installs	Store visits
	Video views	
	Lead generation	

FIGURE 12-3: The first step in the process is choosing your objective.

3. **Choose where you would like to drive traffic. To follow along with the example (and keep things simple), choose Website or Messenger.**

    The Ad Set page appears.

4. **In the Ad Set Name field, type a name for your new ad set.**

    The name should represent your target audience. We entered *Women 30-55 in California,* as shown in Figure 12-4.

5. **In the Locations drop-down (under the Audience heading), do the following:**

    a. *Choose whether you want to include people who live there, have recently been there, or have traveled there.* Most often you want people who live there, but sometimes you might want to target people who have been there recently, such as a promotion to bring them back to your location.

    b. *Type the cities, states, or countries that you are targeting.* You can click the city, state, or country to display a drop-down and slider. Then choose a 10- to 50-mile radius around the city, depending how far from the city's center you want to target.

FIGURE 12-4:
Choose your
audience by
location first.

6. **In the next area, choose the age, gender, and language of the people you're targeting.**

7. **In the Detailed Targeting area, shown in Figure 12-5, choose interests or employers of people that relate to your brand.**

You can also list other Facebook business pages that relate to or compete with yours. For instance, if you own a weight-loss center, you might target people who like the Weight Watchers Facebook business page. You can also exclude people with certain interests or who like certain pages if you think they would be a bad fit for your ad.

8. **(Optional) In the Connections area, add different connection types, such as people who already like your Facebook page.**

9. **Click Save Audience.**

You can use this audience again in future campaigns and avoid the setup process. You are now shown a summary of your choices and are taken to the Placements and Budget & Schedule section.

10. **Choose where you want to run your ad:**

- *To run your ad on Instagram and Facebook:* Choose Automatic Placements.

- *To run your ad only on Instagram:* Deselect everything except Instagram, as shown in Figure 12-6.

FIGURE 12-5:
FIGURE 12-5:
Pinpoint people based on their interests, employers, pages they like, and more.

FIGURE 12-6:
Deselect all options except Instagram if you want to run an Instagram-only campaign.

11. **Scroll down to the Budget & Schedule section, and make your selections.**

You should already have an idea of how much you can spend for the entire campaign, and the length of the campaign.

a. *Choose Daily Budget (the default setting) and enter your daily campaign spending amount in the field.*

Enter the daily amount, not the entire campaign amount.

b. *Choose the days you would like to run the campaign.*

WARNING

12. Click Show Advanced Settings.

13. In the Optimization for Delivery drop-down menu, choose Link Clicks.

Leave all other fields at their default settings.

14. Click Continue.

The Page & Post page appears, with two options: Select an Existing Post and Create New Ad. Carousel ads must be created as a new ad.

15. If you want to use an existing post (on your Facebook business page):

a. *Select Use Existing Post, and then select the Facebook business page that is connected to your Instagram page.*

If you haven't added your Instagram account to Facebook Ads Manager yet (see Figure 12-7), click Add an Account, log in to that account, and accept the request.

b. *Use the Select a Page Post drop-down menu to select the post you want to use, and it appears to the right for your review.* If it is okay as is, click Confirm to submit the ad. If you need to make any changes to it, unfortunately you must edit it on your Facebook business page.

FIGURE 12-7:
To run an ad on your Instagram page, add your official page here using the Add an Account button.

16. If you instead want to create a new ad:

a. *Choose Create New Ad at the top of the Page & Post Page.*

b. *Choose whether you would like to create a carousel, single image, single video, slide show, or collection.*

c. Depending on which option you chose, upload an image, a video, or multiple images and videos.

d. Enter your caption text, choose a call-to-action button, and enter the website in which you'd like to link the ad.

e. Check the preview on the right, and then click Confirm to process the ad.

TIP

If you don't have an Instagram account yet (maybe you are doing your homework first by reading this book), you can use your Facebook business page and it will represent you on Instagram using your Facebook business page name.

Running an Instagram Stories ad in Ads Manager

At the time this book was written, Instagram Stories could be created only in Facebook Ads Manager, not in the mobile app.

To run a Stories ad by using Facebook Ads Manager, follow these steps:

1. **Follow Steps 1-9 in the preceding section on creating a photo, video, or carousel ad.**

2. **In the Placements section, shown in Figure 12-8, select Edit Placements, and then select only Instagram Stories as your placement.**

FIGURE 12-8:
To run an ad in Instagram Stories, deselect every option except Instagram Stories in the Edit Placements area.

○ **Automatic Placements (Recommended)**

Your ads will automatically be shown to your audience in the places they're likely to perform best. For this objective, placements may include Facebook, Instagram, Audience Network and Messenger. Learn more.

● **Edit Placements**

Removing placements may reduce the number of people you reach and may make it less likely that you'll meet your goals. Learn more.

Device Types	All Devices (Recommended) ▼	
Platforms	▶ Facebook	☐
	▼ Instagram	▨
	Feed	☐
	Stories	☑
	▶ Audience Network	☐
	Messenger	☐

---

3. **Scroll down to the Budget & Schedule section.**

   You should already have an idea of how much you can spend for the entire campaign, and the length of the campaign.

4. **Choose Daily Budget (the default setting), enter your daily campaign-spending amount, and choose the days you want to run the campaign.**

   Be sure to enter the daily amount for the campaign, not the entire campaign amount.

WARNING

5. **In the Optimization for Delivery drop-down list, choose Link Clicks.**

   Leave all other fields at their default settings.

6. **Click Continue.**

   The Page & Post page appears, where you can upload your ad. When choosing a Stories ad, you have only one option: Create New Ad.

7. **Upload a photo or an image, or upload a video.**

   Because Stories are vertical, the recommended image size is 1,080 x 1,920 pixels for an image, or filming in the vertical format on your phone for video.

8. **Type your caption text, choose a call-to-action button, and enter the website in which you'd like to link the ad.**

9. **When everything looks good in the preview on the right, click Confirm to process the ad.**

Running an ad in Power Editor

Facebook Power Editor was introduced as a way for larger advertisers to upload and manage multiple ads at once. If you're new to the ad game, we suggest sticking with the easier-to-use Instagram mobile app or Facebook Ads Manager.

If you're confident in your Facebook Ads Manager skills and want to give Power Editor a try, these instructions are for you!

1. **Go to www.facebook.com/poweredtor and click Create Campaign.**

   Unlike Ads Manager, Power Editor doesn't have a drop-down on Facebook. The screen shown in Figure 12-9 appears.

2. **In the first section on the page:**

   a. *In the Campaign Name field, type a campaign name.*

   b. *Leave the Buying Type as Auction so that Facebook will get the best price for your ad.*

   c. *Choose your campaign objective.* You can choose from the following: Brand Awareness, Reach, Traffic, App Installs, Video Views, Lead Generation, Post Engagement, Page Likes, Event Responses, Messages, Conversions, Product Catalog Sales, or Store Visits. To follow along with the example, choose Traffic.

FIGURE 12-9:
Name your campaign, ad set, and ad.

3. **Type a name for your ad set.**

   If you have only one ad set under the campaign name, you can give it the same name as the campaign. If you have multiple ad sets under one campaign, be specific when naming. For example, the campaign might be "Jenni's Thanksgiving Fundraising Campaign," and then the ad set would be a subset that includes targeting, placement, budget, and schedule. You might have several ad sets with different targeting, placement, budget and schedules, but they can all be under the same campaign. (You can go back to Create Campaign at any time and choose Existing Campaign, choose Create New Ad Set, and type a new name.)

4. **Type your ad name.**

   If you have multiple ads under one campaign or ad set, be specific when naming. Similar to the ad set, you can have multiple ad names that can include different pieces of creative or post text.

5. **Click Save to Draft.**

   Another screen pops up confirming your choices and asks for a campaign-spending limit.

6. **Enter your campaign limit, and click the Ad Set Link to the right.**

The next page asks for the same information as the one in Ads Manager.

7. **Complete the information on the Creating the Ad Set page.**

Enter the budget and schedule, locations, age, gender, languages, detailed targeting, and connection types. For detailed information about this section, refer to the directions in Steps 5 through 8 in the "Creating a photo, video, or carousel ad in Ads Manager" section, earlier in this chapter.

8. **Click Save This Audience.**

The next section that appears, Placements, is also the same as the one in Ads Manager.

9. **Decide where to run your ad:**

- *To run the ad on all available ad sections on Instagram and Facebook, leave Automatic Placements selected.*

- *To run the ad only on Instagram, select Edit Placements and deselect everything except Instagram Feed.*

- *To run a Stories ad, select only Instagram Stories.*

10. **In the Optimization & Delivery section, leave everything as automatically selected. Click the 1 Ad link on the top right of the pop-up.**

The Ads page appears.

11. **Make sure the correct Facebook and Instagram accounts are listed in the Identity section.**

If another account appears for Facebook, choose another page in the drop-down list. Take a look at Figure 12-10, which shows the Identity area.

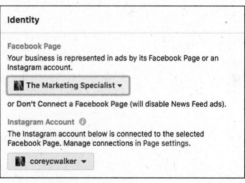

FIGURE 12-10:
Choose the Facebook and Instagram accounts where your ads will be running.

12. **In the next section, choose whether to use an existing post or create an ad:**

- *If you've already created and posted the image and text on Facebook, click Use Existing Post and then choose the post from the Page Post drop-down list. (See Figure 12-11.) The ad appears in the Ad Preview section to the right.*

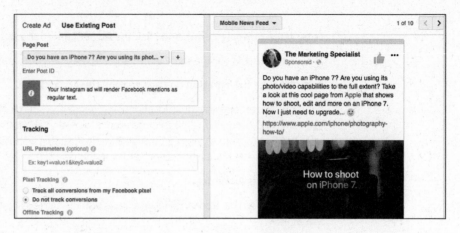

FIGURE 12-11:
You can use an existing Facebook post as an ad.

- *If you want to create the ad in Power Editor, select Create Ad. (See Figure 12-12.) Select one of the three options. From here, you can add images and videos, a website URL, text, a headline, and a newsfeed link description, and choose your call-to-action link. A preview of your ad appears on the right.*

FIGURE 12-12:
Choose the type of ad you're creating.

13. **Click the arrow at the top left of the Create Ad page to go to the main Power Editor dashboard.**

Your ad campaign information is saved as a draft for your review.

14. **Click the blue Review Draft Items button at the top right of the page.**

The Review Draft Items screen appears with the name of your campaign, as shown in Figure 12-13.

15. **Click the green Confirm button.**

If there are no problems, an approval notice appears, and your ad is ready to run! If there are problems, you are notified, along with instructions for correcting them. You can always return to your ad from the dashboard and click Edit to make changes.

Review Draft Items

Select the draft items you want to confirm.

☑ Campaign 1   Ad Set 1   Ad 1

Campaign Name	Change
☑ Instagram for Business for Dummies	NEW

By clicking the "Confirm" button, you agree to Facebook's Terms and Advertising Guidelines.

Cancel   Confirm

FIGURE 12-13:
Power Editor reviews your campaign to check for errors.

TIP

You can make an ad inactive before it's finished running by going to the main dashboard, scrolling to your ad set, and sliding the blue tab to the left of the ad's name, turning it grey.

Monitoring your Instagram ad

After you finish your ad placement, be sure to monitor your Instagram notifications and engage with your audience!

You'll start seeing many more notifications than you normally would — don't ignore them. Tap the heart at the bottom of your screen to see all notifications, and then tap the image from your ad to access your ad's post. From there, you can respond to comments and questions. It may be tempting to tap the heart icon to simply like a comment, but it's best to add a short comment. Doing so makes a difference to the people receiving a personal acknowledgment from you, and it may lead to further conversation about how you or your product might help them.

A/B Testing

After you have designed your first ad and created that perfect caption, you may want to consider A/B testing. In *A/B testing,* you schedule two or more ads, switching one of the ad elements to test which version performs better. In this way, you can hone in on what your audience prefers. Marketers often choose a small budget and time frame to A/B test, and then spend more money and time on the winner of the test.

Here are some examples of A/B tests:

>> Use the same image in two ads, switching out the caption. This could be a complete switch, or you could switch only hashtags, or switch only the call to action, or switch between asking a question and telling users to tag a friend.

>> Use different images in two ads, keeping the same caption.

>> Use the same image and caption, switching the call-to-action ad link from, say, Learn More to Sign Up or Shop Now.

>> Use the same image, caption and call-to-action link, switching your audience to test who responds to the ad more frequently.

Anything that can be swapped out can be tested, but be sure you know the type of results you're looking for. The goal of the test is simply to find the best converting image, caption, call to action, or audience so you can put your ad budget toward the winner.

TIP

Run the test during the same time period with a similar audience if you're testing the ad image, caption, or call-to-action link to prevent seasonality from affecting your results.

You can run the A/B test by scheduling the two ads separately in the Instagram mobile app and then monitoring the results. Creating the ad in the mobile app is discussed in detail previously, in the "Using the Instagram Mobile App to Create an Ad" section, and results measurement is discussed next.

Facebook offers a way to split-test your Instagram ads via the Facebook Ads Manager (see Figure 12-14), but it won't let you A/B test in the ways discussed earlier. The split test uses the same image, caption, and call-to-action link, and then allows you to test the way Facebook delivers it. You can test audiences, optimizations (link clicks versus conversion objectives), or placements (such as running only on Instagram versus only on your Facebook feed or mobile). To split-test an ad in Facebook Ads Manager, click the Split Test box after you've selected your objective and follow the instructions.

Lead generation

Collect lead information from people interested in your business.

☑ **Create Split Test:** Use this ad campaign to test ad set strategies [NEW] ⓘ

Campaign Name ⓘ | Split Test - Lead generation

[Continue]

FIGURE 12-14:
You can split-test your ad.

If you would like to use Ads Manager to A/B test your image, caption, or call-to-action link, you'll need to set up the ads twice in Ads Manager and manually monitor the results.

Measuring Your Ad Results

After you've created and placed an ad, the next task is to measure your ad results. Many businesses overlook this step, but you're smarter than they are! Tracking the effectiveness of a campaign sets you up for future success and saves you money and loads of time. Why would you want to keep running an ad that barely converts to a sale when you could be running a winner?

In this section, you discover how to measure your ad results using Instagram and Facebook Ads Manager.

Viewing Insights via Instagram

Insights include data from your posts about impressions, reach, likes, comments, and more. They are easy to receive via the mobile app. Follow these steps to access them:

1. **On your Instagram profile page, tap the Insights bar graph icon at the top middle of your phone screen.**

2. **Scroll down to the Promotions area, shown in Figure 12-15.**

3. **Click the See More link, if necessary, to see your results.**

    If your promotion is still in progress, you don't need to click the See More link. Any promotions that have run are listed with a thumbnail photo of the ad.

4. **Review the link clicks that your promotion received (listed to the right of the thumbnail) and jot down that information to store with other data later.**

FIGURE 12-15:
The Promotions area of Instagram shows only active campaigns in this area.

5. **Tap anywhere in the field where your promotion is listed to view the ad as it was originally shown to your audience (see Figure 12-16).**

6. **Tap View Results.**

   The Results page appears, as shown in Figure 12-17, with a smaller version of the image, your impressions, reach, likes, comments, and saves. It also displays the total post engagement for your ad versus what one of your typical unpaid posts gets.

FIGURE 12-16:
Instagram shows you what your ad looks like on this screen.

FIGURE 12-17:
The Results page shows you key information about your promotion's performance.

TIP

Now that you've collected this data, store it in a spreadsheet so you can compare it to one of your typical post's results as well as future campaigns. This data is important to use for comparison if you plan on A/B testing other images, captions, text, audiences, or even ad types.

Viewing Insights via Facebook Ads Manager

Ads Manager provides more data on your Instagram ad than Instagram's mobile app. You can see campaign results in Facebook Ads Manager whether you created the ad in Facebook or in Instagram. If you're tracking results closely, Facebook Ads Manager is the better bet because it shows more information about the money you spent and the cost per result. It also allows you to export the data to a .csv or .xls file.

Follow these steps to view your results in Facebook Ads Manager:

1. **Go to Ads Manager by clicking Manage Ads in the drop-down list to the right of your Facebook page or by typing** www.facebook.com/ads/manager.

   All current and completed ads appear on the dashboard.

2. **View a summary of the results by looking to the right of your campaign name, as shown in Figure 12-18.**

   Scroll right to see everything!

FIGURE 12-18:
The Facebook
Ads Manager
dashboard shows
an overview of
your ad's results.

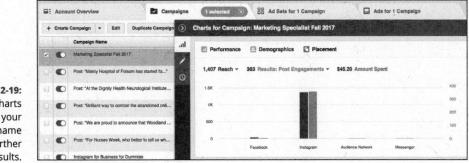

3. **Drill down into the campaign by hovering your cursor over the campaign name and clicking View Charts.**

   Figure 12-19 shows the Charts screen.

FIGURE 12-19:
Click View Charts
under your
campaign name
to see further
campaign results.

4. **Toggle between all three Chart screen options (Performance, Demographics, and Placement) to get the information you need.**

5. **(Optional) To export the results of your campaign:**

   a. *Click the box to the left of your campaign name.*

   b. *At the top right of the screen, under Filters, click Filter by Selection.*

   c. *Click Export.*

   That's all there is to it! Check your web traffic and any other conversions taking place on your website. Include this information with your other Instagram campaign results data so they're part of your final data analysis.

IN THIS CHAPTER

» **Understanding the benefits of contests on Instagram**

» **Learning the rules and regulations for contests**

» **Following the steps to a rewarding contest**

» **Executing a contest successfully**

» **Finalizing the contest**

Chapter **13**

Creating a Winning Contest

Now that you're comfortable with using Instagram, it's time to focus on increasing your audience and creating more results for your business. One of the most effective ways to do this on Instagram is by running contests.

In this chapter, we explain how Instagram contests can be valuable to your business. We also show you the steps to follow to create a successful Instagram contest from start to finish.

Exploring the Benefits of Hosting Instagram Contests

Contests are common on social media, and you've likely seen many of them in your own social media feeds. So many businesses use contests because they know how valuable they are.

Instagram has some of the highest levels of engagement of any social media platform. And running contests or promotions on the platform can drastically increase that engagement for your business. Instagram contests typically require entrants to both like and comment on a photo, thereby increasing engagement on the post.

This increased engagement benefits you: When your followers interact with more of your content, your posts appear higher in their feeds due to the Instagram algorithm.

TECHNICAL
STUFF

Instagram employs an algorithm that sorts through all content created by each person that a user follows. This content is then re-sorted in the user's feed, with the content the user is most likely to engage with near the top of the user's feed. Multiple components affect the algorithm, including how often a user interacts with an account's content, the type of content the user typically interacts with, the time the user spends on Instagram, and a piece's popularity with other users.

We talk more about contest entry requirements later in this chapter. Here, we describe ways that different requirements can benefit your business.

Contests on Instagram often require entrants to follow the account, which increases your followers. In addition, some contests require participants to take a photo and upload it to their account. Each participant sharing content about the company provides reach to new audiences. The company also gets access to a variety of user-generated content that it can repurpose. (For more on user-generated content, see Chapter 8.)

Finally, Instagram contests are simple to implement and administer. This allows you to get many positive results without an overwhelming commitment or cost, increasing your return on investment.

Following the Rules and Restrictions for Running Contests

When running a contest, you need to be aware of several federal and state rules and regulations, far beyond Instagram's requirements. We recommend that you investigate local and national regulations regarding contests, giveaways, promotions, and lotteries before running any contest on social media.

For example, in California, contest and sweepstake laws are defined in CA Bus & Prof Code § 17539. An Internet search for your state's contest or sweepstake laws will help you find the proper rules and regulations. In the US, the Federal Trade

Commission (FTC) regulates disclosure of endorsements (`www.ftc.gov/tips-advice/business-center/guidance/ftcs-endorsement-guides-what-people-are-asking`) and the Federal Communications Commission (FCC) regulates the broadcasting of contests (`www.fcc.gov/consumers/guides/broadcasting-contests-lotteries-and-solicitation-funds` and `www.fcc.gov/general/broadcast-contests`).

While these laws and regulations will give you good guidance, they may be updated or revised at any time. It is always in your best interest to review legal counsel for the most accurate legal advice related to running contests.

Each social media platform has its own rules and restrictions for running contests, and Instagram is no exception. Here, we outline the specific details you need to be aware of for Instagram contests.

WARNING

Although these rules apply at the time this book was published, they can evolve at any point. Read about the current regulations for Instagram contests and promotions at `https://help.instagram.com/179379842258600`.

Listing the official contest rules

Instagram requires that you include the official contest rules in your contest post. These official rules of entry typically include the requirements to enter, the date and time (include the timezone) the contest ends, how winners will be chosen and notified, and any restrictions for entry.

You can simply list these rules of entry directly in your post caption on Instagram. Figure 13-1 is an example of how to format your contest caption to include this information.

If you have more detailed contest rules and terms of entry, or legal disclaimers for your entry requirements, you can include a reference to a website link or a notification to click the link in your profile for full contest rules. Figure 13-2 provides an example of what these more detailed rules and terms of entry might look like.

dinner at two of Nantucket's finest restaurants, the Boarding House and Pearl, a Sailing Cruise on the Endeavor, ice cream from the Juice Bar, provisions from Bartlett's Farm, clothing from In the Pink, North River Outfitter and Vis-a-Vis and organic products from Fare Isle, a nautical doll from Dancey Pants Disco, a one hour film session with Border Free Travels, a tour of the Island and your own Private Concierge from Enjoy Nantucket.

ENTER TO WIN BY FOLLOWING THE STEPS BELOW

1 Follow us and all other hosts of the giveaway
2 "Like" this photo
3 Tap the photo to see where to go next and to see all the great prizes you'll receive. Once you're back here, you've completed the loop 4 Optional: tag a friend you'd take on your ultimate Nantucket Getaway

Rules: Open to to the U.S., Canada AND internationally. Entries to the giveaway will be accepted until 04/13 at 6pm EST. The winner will be chosen at random and announced on 04/14.

Per Instagram rules, we must mention that this is in no way sponsored, administered, or associated with Instagram, Inc. By entering, entrants confirm that they are 13 years of age, release Instagram of responsibility, and agree to Instagram's terms of use.

FIGURE 13-1:
Include your contest rules and terms of entry directly in the post caption.

FIGURE 13-2:
Detailed contest
rules may be
referenced as a
link to a website
or a source for
information.

Releasing Instagram of any involvement

Instagram requires that you include a short paragraph in each contest post that relieves it of any involvement or participation in the contest.

Here is a sample of the verbiage to include, which you can change as needed: "Per Instagram rules, this promotion is in no way sponsored, administered, or associated with Instagram, Inc. By entering, entrants confirm that they are 13+ years of age, release Instagram of responsibility, and agree to Instagram's terms of use."

Planning a Successful Contest

No one wants to put time and energy into something that falls flat on its face or doesn't drive results.

A successful contest on Instagram has the following 11 key components:

>> State your contest goals.

>> Choose a prize.

- » Establish entry requirements.

- » Define rules or conditions.

- » Determine the contest's length.

- » Figure out the promotion schedule.

- » Choose a hashtag.

- » Design the contest's images.

- » Craft post captions.

- » Decide how winners will be chosen and notified.

- » Outline who will respond to contest engagement.

We cover them all in this section so that you'll have the information you need to run a rewarding contest.

Stating your contest goals

Your Instagram contest needs to be designed to serve your business in some way. To successfully execute a contest, you first need to know what you want as a result from the contest.

Businesses typically run a contest for one or more of the following reasons:

- » Increase engagement on their posts

- » Add followers to their Instagram account

- » Increase visits to their website as well as opt-ins or signups for something

- » Gain user-generated content that they can repurpose

It's best to choose one key goal for a single contest, but some companies choose several. For example, more followers might be their primary goal, with increasing engagement as a secondary goal.

After you know why you're running your contest, you're ready to move on with planning.

Choosing a prize

To get people to participate, you have to provide something of value that they would like to win. Prizes can range from low value to extremely high value, depending on your resources and goals.

TIP

Your prize should always be related to your business! Giving away an iPad or other generic prize doesn't attract your ideal audience and creates unnecessary interest in your contest. Instead, choose one or your own products or services that would appeal to your target audience.

Your prize should be commensurate with the level of participation to enter. For example, if the prize is valued at $10, a simple "like a photo" contest is appropriate. By comparison, asking people to take a photo, post it to their account, and use your hashtag to promote you requires a considerable amount of work and effort, so the prize should be significantly more valuable.

You also need to decide how many winners will be awarded. Will more than one person win the same prize? Or will one winner get the grand prize and one or more additional winners receive a smaller prize? If you want to offer different levels of prizes, you need to determine what they are.

Establishing entry requirements

To be entered into the contest, participants have to do something. Some of the most common entry requirements follow:

>> Following your account

>> Liking the photo you posted

>> Mentioning one or more people in the comments

>> Posting a photo with a specific hashtag

>> Filling out a form on your website

You may even choose to have them complete two or three of these requirements as a full entry into the contest. Figure 13-3 shows one contest that requires multiple components to enter.

TIP

It's best to limit the number of criteria for entry to two or three steps. The more complicated you make the entry process, the fewer participants.

View Insights

Promote

Liked by **watsonks, stephanie.carls** and **91 others**
jenns_trends Join me to win a 30 minute consultation! Here's how to enter: ⭐ Attend my LIVE session at #HUG17 at 4:15 pm on Thursday, February 2nd.
⭐ Take a photo during the live session - creativity helps! Upload the image to Instagram by Saturday, February 4th.
⭐ TAG me (not @ mention) in the photo and use both hashtags #LearnFromJenn and #HUG17

Entries accepted until Saturday, February 4, 2017. Entries open to attendees of the live event on February 2, 2017. Entrant profile must be public.

Winner will be announced on Monday, February 6, 2017. One winner will be chosen.

Per Instagram rules, this is in no way sponsored, administered, or associated with Instagram, Inc. By entering, entrants confirm they are 13+ years of age, release Instagram of responsibility, and agree to Instagram's terms of use.

FIGURE 13-3:
A contest may include multiple criteria to submit a complete entry.

Defining the rules or conditions

We mentioned Instagram's contest rules, as well as the need to follow any local, state, and federal regulations. You also need to determine your own rules for entry.

Add any criteria related to age restrictions, geographical restrictions, content to be shared in photographs, and limits to quantities awarded in the contest.

Determining the contest's length

You have many things to consider when determining the length of your contest. The first factor is how many days or weeks the contest will run. Typically, for the best performance, contests that are longer than 3 days and less than 2 weeks are best.

For contests that require entrants to post a photo or create content, it's best to let the contest run longer in order to give them time to create and upload their entries.

Knowing your contest duration, you then need to determine the exact day and time the contest will both begin and end so that you can include this in your contest details and your planning calendar.

Figuring out the promotion schedule

Now that you know how long the contest will run and when it will start and end, you need to determine how often you will promote the contest on Instagram.

You always want to promote the contest on the first day and then again on the last day to remind people to enter before time runs out. Depending on the length of the contest, however, you might want to promote the contest also one or more times throughout to keep momentum and to reach more people.

Choosing a hashtag

It's advantageous to use a unique hashtag for each contest because it helps you track the contest on Instagram and allows your audience to easily participate.

When every participant uses the same hashtag to identify his or her post or entry, you can view the submissions in the hashtag search gallery on Instagram or by using a third-party tool such as Tagboard (http://tagboard.com).

Having a unique hashtag for each contest also allows you to monitor participation in each contest and compare those contests to determine which ones perform best or drive the best engagement.

Choosing the right hashtag may take a little time. When selecting your contest hashtag, consider the following:

>> The hashtag should be unique to the individual contest.

>> The hashtag should be related to your brand or the specific topic of the contest or both.

>> The hashtag can be longer than usual to add distinguishing context.

Figure 13-4 shows three examples of unique hashtags that different accounts utilized in their contests. You can see how each one used a hashtag related to the contest theme.

FIGURE 13-4:
Contest hashtags for different brands demonstrate the unique qualities of each contest.

TIP

Include your contest hashtag as a text overlay on the images promoting the contest. Doing so will make the post image stand out on Instagram and build awareness of the contest.

Designing contest images

To promote your contest on Instagram in accordance with the schedule you determined in the previous steps, you need to create at least one image to post as the contest notification. You can create more than one image to keep the momentum going and content fresh in the Instagram feed.

The images should be related to the contest's theme. For example, if you're creating a back-to-school contest, your post image might be school supplies or an apple on a teacher's desk. The images should set the tone for the theme and the purpose of the contest, as shown in Figure 13-5.

One of the images may also include an example or preview of the prize. For example, if the prize is a box of your products, a well-staged photo of the box and its components will get your audience excited for what they could win and help encourage them to participate.

REMEMBER

You can also include a text box or text details on your image to highlight the contest or provide contest details. In Figure 13-4, the @Petco contest post includes details about the dates, the prize, and the contest hashtag.

FIGURE 13-5:
Your images should match the theme of your contest.

Crafting post captions for the contest

Your post caption should let people know you are running a contest and also get them excited about the contest and encourage them to participate. Write a post caption for each post of the contest in advance. This enables you to share a cohesive message throughout the contest and ensures that you don't omit necessary or important information.

TIP

If you plan to run contests frequently, draft a caption template for contest posts and save it on your mobile device. This way, you can open it each time you plan to run a contest, and update the information for the current contest details.

Your caption should include the following:

>> A statement that you are running a contest

>> Prize details

>> Your contest entry requirements

>> Legal disclosures

We talk about the legal disclosure requirements previously in this chapter. You want to include all those details in your post captions.

Refer to Figures 13-1 and 13-3 for great examples of incorporating all these details into a contest caption.

Deciding how winners will be chosen and notified

How you will determine winners depends on how the contest was structured and how the entries were submitted. The two most common ways to choose a winner are using judges and through random selection.

If your plan is to have someone judge the entries to determine a winner, you need to clearly state the winning criteria. For example, if you require entrants to submit photos of their pets with your product, two obvious criteria are that the photo must include both a pet and your product. Additional criteria may include creativity, unique animals, or content that is most closely aligned with your brand theme and styling.

After you decide how the winners will be chosen, outline how you will notify them. It's best to notify the winners directly and privately first. You can do this by sending them a direct message on Instagram (see Chapter 6 for details on direct messaging). Or if they submitted entries by including an email address, you can email their notification. You might also post a comment on their original post on their Instagram account, if that's an option.

After you notify the winners privately, you might want to post something on your Instagram account, announcing the winners of the contest. This step isn't necessary and many brands do not do this. For smaller brands, however, the transparency of announcing winners can build trust with your audience that you are actually awarding prizes to real people.

Outlining who will respond to contest engagement

If you're the only one managing your Instagram account, all contest management will fall on you. If you have more than one person on your team, though, clearly outline who is responsible for reviewing and responding to contest engagement.

Throughout the contest, people will request clarification about entry requirements, ask about the prize, or otherwise want more information on the contest. Someone on your team must be able to respond to these questions quickly and accurately.

You also need someone to monitor the entrants and ensure that they are valid entries. Depending on the entrant requirements you established, this task might include the following:

>> Monitoring your post for comments and usernames listed in the comments

>> Monitoring the contest hashtag for post entries made on participants' accounts

>> Verifying that each entrant is, in fact, following your account

Monitoring and validating are time-consuming. Be sure to factor in enough time to review entrants before announcing a winner.

Executing a Winning Contest

Now that you have everything in place to run the contest successfully, it's time to execute it.

If you've completed all the prepatory steps outlined in this chapter, the contest execution will be fairly smooth. However, things can always pop up or go unexpectedly, so be prepared to be flexible throughout the contest period.

The first thing to do is to post your first contest announcement image and caption, based on the timeline you established for the contest. After that post goes up on Instagram, actively cross-promote the contest to your audience. Share the contest image to other social media sites for your business and encourage those followers to join you on Instagram to enter the contest. Send an email to your email list, informing the recipients about the contest and asking them to submit their entry on Instagram. If you have a physical business location, encourage your customers who come in to participate as well.

As the contest gets going, ensure that you are monitoring and readily responding to comments and questions.

In accordance with the contest time frame you established, post subsequent contest posts and reminders to your Instagram account throughout the duration of the contest. Post your final contest post on the last day of the contest and get ready to wrap it up!

Following Up

After the contest has reached the end date and time, you need to close out the contest, announce the winners, and review the entire contest.

TIP

After the contest is officially closed, go back to your contest posts on Instagram and edit the caption to add "Contest Closed" or a similar statement at the top of the caption. This ensures that anyone reading your post after the contest entry period understands that the contest is over and won't attempt to participate.

Now that you have all your entrants, you need to select a winner. Whether you're selecting a randomly generated winner or having the entries judged, choose your individual winner, multiple winner, or winners for different prize levels.

Next, you have to notify the winners. Follow the plan you put in place to notify them directly first. Then make a public post on your profile, if you choose to do so, announcing the winners.

If you must deliver prizes to the winners, coordinate the delivery with them. Do so through private messaging or email communications.

TIP

If you're shipping winners a physical package, send them the tracking number of the package so that they can confirm when it will arrive.

After the contest is completed, review your contest analytics. Some of the information to review and measure follows:

>> Number of new followers on your Instagram account

>> Number of people who participated

>> Number of likes and comments on your contest posts

>> Amount of traffic generated to your website during the contest period

>> Number of conversions through opt-ins or sales during the contest or as a result of the contest

To determine what contest strategies and tactics performed best for you and your business, compare the results from multiple contests. Each time you run a contest, track the analytics just mentioned and compare them to previous contests.

See if the following factors contributed to an increase in participation or conversions:

>> Duration of the contest

>> Number of posts promoting the contest

>> Prize

>> Types of images promoting the contest

Contests on Instagram can provide big benefits when executed properly. Remember, though, that time and repeated contests are necessary to deliver significant results. This is why it helps to plan and to track each contest.

Chapter **14**

Connecting Your Marketing Dots

I f you've read any of the previous chapters, you've already discovered many expert tips for using Instagram for your business. However, most people who have success with Instagram don't use it in a vacuum. It's important to know where and how to place Instagram in your total marketing mix to get the best results. In this chapter, we discuss incorporating Instagram with your other social media, website, and offline activities, as well as how to monitor your Instagram stats to ensure that you're on the right track.

Incorporating Instagram in Your Marketing Mix

Let's face it, Instagram *is* awesome, right? We sure think so. But it should be just one of many tactics in your marketing plan. Businesses that are truly successful use Instagram as part of their overall mix, not as their entire focus.

Here are some other marketing avenues to consider:

>> Facebook, Twitter, LinkedIn, Pinterest, Google+, and YouTube

>> Email and blogs

>> Webinars

>> SEO

>> Google AdWords

>> Review sites such as Yelp, Angie's List, and TripAdvisor

>> Industry forums, conferences, speaking engagements, and events

>> Local events (chamber, rotary, neighborhood)

>> One-on-one appointments

>> Direct mail and telesales

That list is not all encompassing, but we hope it gets you brainstorming. Your industry or company may offer more ways to market your business. The most important point is to choose the best vehicles for the audience you're trying to reach. Instagram may be the perfect target, but you can get Instagram traffic from other places, online and offline. Let's get started!

Connecting Instagram to Other Social Networks

An easy way to get more Instagram content views is to connect your other social networks to your Instagram account. Currently, the US-based networks that you can link to Instagram are Facebook, Twitter, and Tumblr. Adding linked accounts is a snap:

1. **From your Instagram profile page, tap the gear icon, which is next to the Edit Profile button.**

   The Options page appears.

2. **Scroll down to Settings and tap Linked Accounts (see Figure 14-1, left).**

   The Share Settings screen appears, as shown in Figure 14-1, right.

3. **Tap Facebook.**

4. **Authorize Instagram to share photos on your Facebook page.**

   You're automatically redirected back to the Share Settings page in Instagram. Note that the Facebook icon has changed from gray to blue, now that it's linked.

5. **Repeat this process for all other networks that you want to link to Instagram.**

6. **To return to your profile page, tap your profile picture at the bottom right of the screen.**

FIGURE 14-1: Access Linked Accounts from the Options page (left), and then use the Share Settings page to connect Instagram with Facebook, Twitter, or Tumblr (right).

After you save the Linked Accounts settings, you won't need to touch that area again unless you want to add another social network. You can now share an image or video that you post on Instagram directly to the other networks you set up. Here's how:

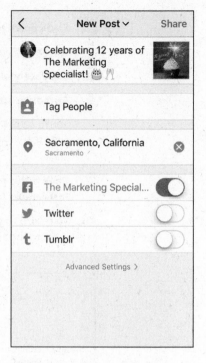

FIGURE 14-2:
Share your Instagram post to other platforms by tapping the appropriate social network tab.

1. **Upload your image or video along with a caption as you would for a normal post.**

2. **If you would like to tag people or add a location, do that next.**

3. **At the bottom of the page, tap the slider to move it to the right for each network to which you want to post your Instagram post.**

   The tab for each selected network turns blue. See Figure 14-2.

4. **Tap Share at the top of the screen.**

   The post goes to Instagram and any other network you selected.

That's it!

Including Instagram on Your Website

You can incorporate Instagram directly on your website in several ways. The main three tactics we discuss are as follows:

>> Linking a button on your website to Instagram

>> Allowing users to share your articles or blog posts on their social media accounts

>> Embedding your Instagram feed on your website

TIP

Exact instructions for adding these items to your website may differ depending on how your website was built. If you did not build your website, ask your webmaster for help if needed.

Linking your website to your Instagram page

If you have a website, all your business's social networks should be linked to your website so your prospective customers can easily find and follow you on Instagram, Facebook, and more. See Figure 14-3 for an example. Most website builders, such as Wix, SquareSpace, and GoDaddy, offer a variety of social media icons that you can easily drop in. For Instagram specifically, you need to link the icon to your Instagram web address: `http://www.instagram.com/` *yourusername.*

FIGURE 14-3:
Add links to your social media profile on your website.

If your website was not built on a website builder platform, you can still add a link to Instagram. Here's how:

1. **Do a Google search for an Instagram icon available for downloading.**

   Many are available for free.

2. **Download the icon that best fits your website's design, and save it to your computer.**

3. **Go to your website's content management system or backend.**

   Details for this process are beyond the scope of the book. Consult your webmaster for help if needed.

4. **Add the Instagram social media icon to your page as you would for any other image.**

5. **Link the Instagram icon to** `http://www.instagram.com/`*yourusername.*

That's all there is to it. Repeat the process for all active business social media accounts.

TIP

Make sure you size the social media icons correctly (all the same size, not too large or small) before you upload them to your site. The standard size for social media icons is 32 x 32 pixels.

Allowing others to share your content via Instagram

You've likely noticed and used social media share buttons, which typically appear at the top or bottom of a web article or blog, as shown in Figure 14-4. Share buttons enable you to share that content via your Facebook, Twitter, LinkedIn, Pinterest, and several other social networks — except Instagram. Unfortunately, Instagram's current terms of service do not allow you to add a Share This button on your website.

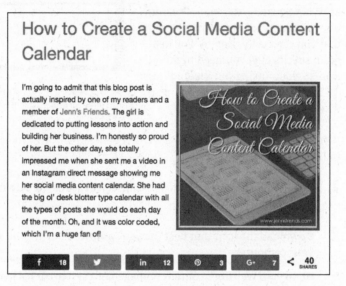

FIGURE 14-4:
Social media share buttons for a variety of networks are available at the bottom of this web article.

We still encourage you to add your other social networks to further your content reach. Most website builders have share button widgets so you can easily share your content. If you have a custom website, here are some websites that work similarly and offer share button solutions at no or low monthly costs:

» AddThis, at www.addthis.com

» AddToAny, at www.addtoany.com

» ShareThis, at www.sharethis.com

Embedding your Instagram feed on your website

Looking to entice your website viewers to check out your Instagram profile? Add your Instagram feed to one of your website's pages, as shown in Figure 14-5. Users click an individual image to be taken to that image on your Instagram profile. It's a great way to tempt people to go to your account.

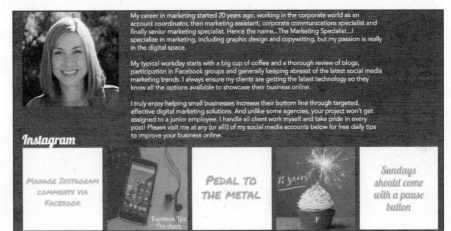

FIGURE 14-5: This website has its Instagram feed embedded on one of its web pages.

TIP

Before you embed your Instagram feed on your website, think through your strategy. Would you rather have your audience stay on your website or go over to Instagram? Make sure you aren't luring them away from the place you want them to be!

Similar to the social media icons discussed earlier in this section, many website builder companies offer widgets or apps to easily insert your Instagram feed on your website. Follow their instructions for adding the Instagram feed widget. You'll need to know your Instagram web address for this task (http://www.instagram.com/*yourusername*).

If you have a custom or WordPress website, you can add the Instagram feed by using one of several widgets, such as the following:

>> Juicer, at www.juicer.io

>> POWr, at www.powr.io/plugins/instagram-feed

>> SnapWidget, at https://snapwidget.com/

All three have free options for smaller accounts and follow similar directions:

1. **Sign up on their website by providing an email and password.**

2. **Choose Instagram as the social media network.**

3. **Sign in to your Instagram account and allow the app to access your account.**

4. **Provide your Instagram account's web address:** `http://www.instagram.com/yourusername.`

5. **Click Embed in Your Site (or something similar, such as Generate Embed Code) to generate the embed code.**

6. **Copy and paste the embed code on the backend of your website on the web page where you would like the feed to appear.**

TIP

If you're unfamiliar with your website's HTML code, provide the embed code to your webmaster to copy and paste in the correct spot on your website.

Promoting Instagram on Printed Materials

It's handy to use online methods to send prospective customers to Instagram because they can easily click through to your profile. However, it's still important to advertise your account on printed materials, as shown in Figure 14-6. You never know when a flyer or brochure might be someone's ticket to visiting your Instagram account.

FIGURE 14-6:
The bottom of this flyer shows several ways to contact the business, including through Instagram.

Use the official Instagram icon (a high-resolution icon is available for free download at `https://en.instagram-brand.com/`) along with *@yourusername* on printed items such as the following:

>> Business cards

>> Postcards

>> Flyers

>> Brochures

>> Posters

>> In-store signage

TIP

Make sure any social media icons you use are high-resolution files that will print correctly. Never use blurry or pixelated icons. If you need help creating your print materials, hire an experienced graphic designer.

Incorporate the Instagram logo and your username as often as you can to remind potential customers to find you there. In the next section, we discuss how you can integrate Instagram into your promotions, both online *and* offline.

Incorporating Instagram into an Event or Promotion

If you have an upcoming event or promotion, Instagram can be a fabulous way to advertise. Before going too far into this section, we recommend you read Chapter 13 thoroughly first. All the legal details and do's and don'ts for Instagram contests are covered there.

After you know the ins and outs of running a contest on Instagram, it's time to look at it from a slightly different angle. Sometimes you can use Instagram as a supplement to other marketing tactics such as email marketing or direct mail to promote your event or promotion.

Here are some ways you can use Instagram to increase attendance at an event:

>> Create an official event hashtag for consistent use throughout the event's promotion and the event itself. (See Chapter 8 for details on using hashtags.)

>> Create custom graphics with text overlays announcing the event, and provide the details in the caption, as shown in Figure 14-7. Use the link in your profile bio as a link to more information or registration. Tell people to comment if they are participating, and tag a friend who might also like to participate.

>> Post photos or videos of certain aspects of the event, such as speakers, special guests, and fun activities, as shown in Figure 14-8.

>> Post behind-the-scenes photos or videos of event prep, such as putting together hundreds of swag bags, setting up decorations, or late-night pizza sessions after burning the midnight oil.

>> Post posters, purchase space on a billboard, or hire a van advertised with your event to drive around town. Have clear instructions asking people to take a photo of the ad and upload it to their Instagram account using the event hashtag.

>> Use an influencer in your industry to help spread the word about your event. Be prepared to pay for this!

>> Ask people to post a photo or video that relates to your event (user-generated content) using the event hashtag for a chance to win free tickets to the event.

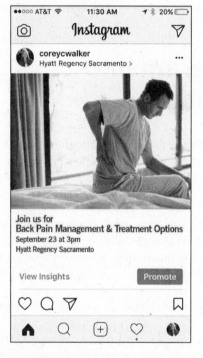

FIGURE 14-7:
Custom graphics with text overlays can be helpful when announcing an event on Instagram.

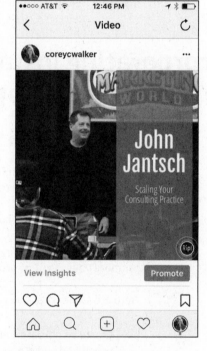

FIGURE 14-8:
Posting photos of featured speakers can get people excited about an upcoming event.

To increase the reach of your event posts, use Instagram ads. You can target a specific audience rather than just those who are currently following you. For more information about Instagram planning and creating ads, read Chapters 11 and 12, respectively.

At the event, use signs like those in Figure 14-9, asking people to upload photos of the event using the event hashtag. Repost their photos, making sure you appropriately tag them and give them photo credit.

You should also designate or hire an official photographer to ensure that you get quality photos of all major aspects of the event. Posting these photos at the beginning of the event can generate more attendees on-the-fly if your event accepts last-minute walk-ins. Post more photos the following week to keep the buzz going about your brand. And if you hold the event annually, you can use those photos also to promote the event the next year.

Aside from events, Instagram can be used to promote a promotion, such as a flash sale at your store or product giveaway:

FIGURE 14-9:
Include signs with your event hashtag to encourage people to post photos during the event.

>> Similar to promoting an event, post custom graphics with text overlays announcing the promotion and provide details in the caption, as shown in Figure 14-10. The link in your bio can link to more information or a sales page.

>> Ask Instagram followers to repost your promotion post and tag you in exchange for a reduction in the price of the product or service.

>> Create an Instagram-exclusive deal in which you provide a discount or coupon code only to people who view the deal on Instagram. This approach provides an easy way to track people who are coming from this network versus others.

>> Message new followers of your page with a free gift or discount on your products or services.

>> Ask Instagram followers to post a photo or video of your product, tagging you and using the specified hashtag, to receive a gift or product discount.

>> Use an influencer in your industry or someone your audience would recognize, to promote your sale. Have that person offer a unique discount code so you can track the tactic's effectiveness.

>> Use Instagram Stories to offer 24-hour-only specials, as shown in Figure 14-11. Post a notice in your store, in your email newsletters, and on your website to let your customers know about these flash specials.

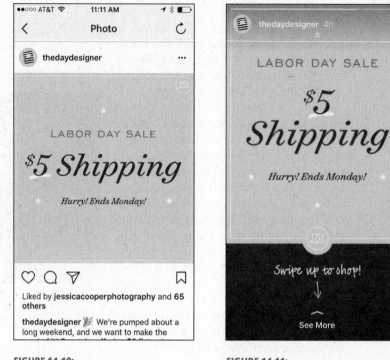

FIGURE 14-10:
Custom graphics with text overlays can call attention to your promotion.

FIGURE 14-11:
Instagram Stories are the perfect place to post 24-hour specials because the story automatically disappears after 24 hours.

Monitoring Your Instagram Stats

Any good marketer knows that analytics are a huge key to your marketing success. By monitoring follower growth, engagement (likes, mentions, and comments), website clicks, and branded hashtag growth, you can track what's working and do more of it. And you can stop doing the tactics that aren't working too!

If you have an Instagram business profile, Instagram offers basic and easy to access insights through the mobile app. In addition, several third-party apps allow you to dig a little deeper than what Instagram offers. We go over both types in this section.

Using Instagram's native analytics

As mentioned, Instagram offers several insights to track your Instagram success by using the mobile app. To begin, tap the bar graph at the top right of your Instagram profile page on your phone, as shown in Figure 14-12. When you do, the Insights page shown in Figure 14-13 appears.

FIGURE 14-12:
The Instagram Insights icon is located at the top right of your profile page.

FIGURE 14-13:
The Insights page displays results from the past week for your Instagram business account.

On the Insights page, you see the following data about your account:

>> Number of impressions (number of times your account has been seen) for the last seven days. Swipe left to see Reach.

>> Reach (number of unique accounts that saw your account) for the last seven days. Swipe left to see Profile Views.

>> Profile views for the last seven days.

>> Posts in the last seven days ranked by highest impressions. Posts are all clickable for more data. Tap See More to see all your posts from the last year, ranked by highest impressions.

>> Stories in the last 7 days ranked by highest impressions. Tap See More to see the impressions of all stories posted in the last 14 days.

>> Times of day (for the current day) when your followers are most active. Tap See More for more information about how many followers you have and their demographics (gender, age, and location).

>> Active promotion results. Tap See More to view past completed promotions and their results, including impressions, reach, likes, comments, and total post engagement.

Depending on your Instagram goals, you may choose to track some or all of these analytics. Some easy metrics to track are follower growth, impressions growth, and which posts and stories are getting the best engagement. A simple Excel spreadsheet updated weekly, like the one in Figure 14-14, may be all you need to notice trends and make adjustments to your tactics and post styles.

Week	Followers	Impressions	Best Post	B. Post Impressions	B. Post Likes	B. Post Comments	Best Story	Story Impressions	Story Messages	Notes
Feb 5-11, 2018	5,667	4,555	Sunflower girl	800	189	13	Dancing sunflower	98	5	
Feb 12-18, 2018	5,779	4,676	Computer screen	855	226	17	BTS of graphic design	102	3	
Feb 19-25, 2018	5,899	4,578	25% Sale promo	999	207	14	25% off Boomerang	122	8	#beautysale
Sept 20-26, 2018	6,005	4,699	Selfie w/dog	1,200	345	22	Dog begging	300	13	dogpark location

In the next section, we discuss various third-party applications that can be used to track your Instagram data.

Best third-party apps for Instagram analytics

Instagram's Insights are a great tool for providing an overall view of how your account and posts are performing. However, a number of other analytics tools can help you dive deeper for more in-depth data. In this section, we discuss three popular third-party analytics apps: Iconosquare, Simply Measured, and Sprout Social.

Iconosquare

If you are into Instagram more than any other social media network, Iconosquare might be a great fit for you. Iconosquare offers analytics and content management for Instagram only. Its strong suit is analytics, but it is also a robust content management system that enables you to research hashtags, upload content, schedule content, and sort your content later by topic.

The analytics area, which is shown in Figure 14-15, is where you can see detailed data about your Instagram account. Iconosquare offers all the standard data that Instagram Insights offers, plus the following:

>> Daily gained and lost followers

>> Comparisons about your post's real-time performance versus previous posts

>> Performance on each of your hashtags and various other ways to see data about what areas of the world are using your hashtags and at what time

>> Performance based on the filter used

>> Comparison of your performance versus your competitors' performance

You can also handpick which data you'd like exported into a report, which can be a huge timesaver versus creating your own spreadsheet.

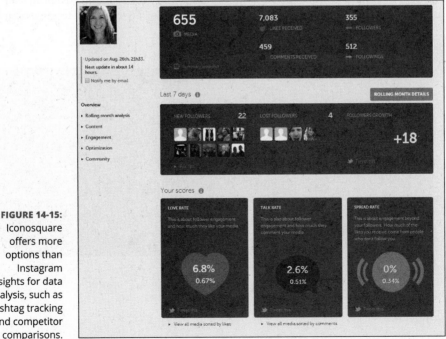

FIGURE 14-15: Iconosquare offers more options than Instagram Insights for data analysis, such as hashtag tracking and competitor comparisons.

Iconosquare is a paid subscription app, with costs ranging from $108/year for basic functions (which you can get free on Instagram Insights) to $948/year for more advanced functions for marketing teams. To get information on current offerings and pricing, visit `https://pro.iconosquare.com/`.

Simply Measured

Even more robust than Iconosquare, Simply Measured offers all the tools in Instagram Insights as well as these large segments:

- » **Listening:** Identify influencers, better understand your target audience and learn more about who is talking about your brand.

- » **Social analytics:** Track comments, likes, shares, and overall engagement in an environment that can be filtered and exported easily into a report.

- » **Content share tracking:** View which of your URLs are being shared via social media, and track web page bounces and time spent by visitors on your website.

- » **Conversion tracking:** Tracks actions on your social posts all the way through to the end action, such as a purchase or registration.

Simply Measured offers analytics on Instagram, Twitter, Facebook, Pinterest, LinkedIn, and YouTube but doesn't offer content management or scheduling components. It is strictly for analytics and is a great tool for an advanced user who is highly focused on the return on investment. See Figure 14-16 for an example of its interface.

FIGURE 14-16: Simply Measured offers high-level analytics for advanced marketers.

Simply Measured is a paid subscription app that starts at $500/month. It is used by large corporations or small businesses that are highly in tune with their marketing data. It does have free analytics tools available at `https://simplymeasured.com/free-social-media-tools/`, if you'd like to check there first. To learn more about Simply Measured, visit `https://simplymeasured.com/`.

Sprout Social

If you want one app to do everything — including content creation and management, scheduling, analytics, and reporting for most of the major social media networks — Sprout Social has you covered. The Sprout Social dashboard is shown in Figure 14-17.

Sprout Social offers the following services (and more) for Instagram, Facebook, Twitter, LinkedIn, and YouTube:

>> Plan, schedule, and post messages

>> Store content for later use

>> Edit images with filters or text overlays

>> Suggest optimal send times

>> Track post performance by likes, shares, and comments

>> Track campaign URLs for referral traffic and conversions

>> Watch Instagram follower growth

>> Compare Instagram profiles with competitors

>> Identify key influencers for your brand

>> Track and report hashtags

>> Unlimited exports of reports and PDFs

Sprout Social starts at $99/month, which does not include all features. For full pricing and detailed information about which analytics offerings are included in each pricing tier, visit `https://sproutsocial.com`.

FIGURE 14-17:
The Sprout Social dashboard offers easy-to-understand reporting for Instagram and most other social media networks.

Before investing in a monthly or yearly analytics package for any of the third-party apps, research which data you think you'll need. Third-party apps have a lot of extra bells and whistles, but if you aren't going to use them, you're wasting money. We suggest that you use the free analytics provided by the Instagram app first to see whether they give you enough data to evaluate your results, and then decide whether you need more information from a paid app.

5

Why Isn't This Working?

IN THIS PART . . .

Find relief for common issues when you use the Instagram app.

Join a community for Instagram support, moral and otherwise.

Chapter 15

Insta-Diagnosing Instagram

Nothing in this world is perfect, and Instagram is no different. Sometimes weird (and frustrating) quirks happen with the app and you may find it difficult to do certain things while using it. Have no fear, though! Help is on the way . . . just keep reading.

In this chapter, we take you through some of the more common issues that users report running into with Instagram and give you steps to correct (or at least get past) them.

REMEMBER

The latest versions of iOS for the iPhone and iPad (version 11.0.2) and Android (version 7.0) were used to create the instructions for this chapter. If you have an older version of iOS or Android, your mileage may vary.

Installation Issues

When Instagram won't install for you, we've got your back. Instead of panicking, read on to discover the common reasons why Instagram won't install and suggestions for resolving them. If they don't work, take a few deep breaths because we've thought of that, too, in the "Nothing Is Working . . . Now What?" section, later in the chapter.

Dealing with compatibility issues

If you're receiving compatibility error messages, it may be time for you to upgrade your operating system before you install Instagram because the app requires iOS 8 or later on an iPhone or iPad.

For Android users, the Google Play Store entry for Instagram states that compatibility is dependent on the smartphone or tablet you're using. When you download Instagram, the Google Play Store automatically checks your smartphone or tablet to ensure that it's compatible.

That said, Instagram notes that some Android users receive a "Device not compatible" message. If you receive this message, Instagram recommends that you clear all Google Play Store data stored on your smartphone or tablet and then try to install Instagram again. (As of this writing, Instagram says it's investigating this issue with Google. By the time you read this, we hope the issue is resolved.)

Here's how to clear all Google Play Store data from your Android device:

1. **In a home screen or the Apps screen, tap the Settings icon.**

2. **Tap Applications.**

3. **Swipe up and tap Google Play Store in the All Apps list.**

   The Application Info screen appears.

4. **Tap Storage.**

   The Storage screen appears, as show in Figure 15-1.

5. **Tap the Clear Data button.**

6. **Tap Delete in the pop-up window that appears.**

Now you can return to the Google Play Store and try to install Instagram again. If that doesn't work, check out Chapter 16 for information on support from Instagram and other online sources.

FIGURE 15-1:
Clear your Google Play Store data here.

Checking your space

If you use your smartphone or tablet a lot, you know that storage issues are a bane of your existence. (If it's your only bane, well done.) You can check the memory usage to see how much memory space Instagram is eating up.

iPhone and iPad

It's easy to find out how much storage space Instagram is using on your iPhone or iPad:

1. **On your home screen, tap Settings.**

2. **Swipe up on the screen if necessary, and then tap General in the settings list.**

   The General screen appears.

3. **Tap iPhone Storage or iPad Storage.**

   The iPhone Storage or iPad Storage screen appears.

4. **Tap Instagram. (You may need to swipe up first.)**

   In the Info screen that appears, the Documents & Data entry shows you how much storage space Instagram is using, as shown in Figure 15-2.

FIGURE 15-2:
The storage space that the Instagram app is taking up appears to the right of the Documents & Data entry.

TIP

If you think Instagram is taking up too much space and the app is affecting the performance of your iPhone or iPad, tap Offload App to free up storage space but save your photos and profile data. If that doesn't help, reinstalling Instagram might. Instagram will save your data so that everything will still be there when you reinstall.

To reinstall Instagram, tap Delete App in the Info screen. Then repeat the steps in this section to see whether reinstalling freed up any storage space.

Android smartphone and tablet

As with the iPhone and iPad, it's easy to find out how much memory the Instagram app is using on your Android smartphone or tablet. Here's how:

1. **On a home screen or the Apps screen, tap Settings.**

   The Settings screen appears.

2. **Tap Applications.**

3. **Swipe up until you see the Instagram entry in the All Apps list.**

4. **Tap Instagram.**

   The Application Info screen appears.

5. **Tap Storage.**

   The total storage appears in the Storage screen, as shown in Figure 15-3.

To clear all the memory that the Instagram app is using without clearing all the app's data, tap the Clear Cache button.

FIGURE 15-3:
The storage space on an Android device.

If you think Instagram is taking up too much space and the app is affecting the performance of your smartphone or tablet, tap the Clear Data button in the Storage screen. Then tap Delete in the pop-up window that appears in the center of the screen.

Android clears your Instagram profile data stored on your smartphone or tablet, any photos or videos you've taken in the Instagram app that you haven't posted to your feed, as well as all the memory that the Instagram app is using. If the app is open, it closes automatically.

REMEMBER

If you've already posted photos or videos to your Instagram account, your posts remain in your feed. Photos and videos you've saved on your smartphone or tablet are also safe.

AT&T ⚹ 🔋 98% 3:34 AM

< STORAGE

Instagram

STORAGE

Total 67.11 MB
App 58.27 MB
Data 8.84 MB

CLEAR DATA

Cache 104 MB

CLEAR CACHE

Unfreezing an installation on your iPhone or iPad

If the Instagram app freezes during installation and you've given the App Store a reasonable amount of time to install the app, try a cold restart of your iPhone or iPad by turning the device off and then back on.

After you restart your iPhone or iPad, try installing the Instagram app once more. If this doesn't work, you'll have to contact Apple support, which is easy to access from the Apple website. Once on the website, click or tap the Support option at the top of the screen. On your iPhone, tap the menu icon in the upper-left corner of the page and then tap Support.

Finding a missing app on your iPhone or iPad

If the App Store says Instagram is installed but you don't see it on your iPhone or iPad, connect your phone to your computer and sync your apps using the iTunes program on your computer.

If iTunes won't cooperate, it's time to contact Apple support on its website.

Resolving issues on an Android device

If you have problems installing the Instagram app on an Android device, there may be a connectivity problem between the Google Play Store and your smartphone or tablet.

In this case, you'll need to go through the Google Play troubleshooting wizard, which will take you step-by-step through solving the problem. If the wizard can't help, Google will give you options for contacting its support staff members so they can dig deeper. You can access the wizard at https://support.google.com/googleplay/troubleshooter/6241347?hl=en.

Log-In Difficulties

If you can't log in to the Instagram app, one of several issues may be the culprit. You may have a problem with your username or password, or Instagram may have disabled your account. We'll be your guide in resolving all these problems so you can start Instagramming.

Checking your username

If Instagram won't accept your username, you may have typed the username incorrectly. This may seem silly or even insulting, but ensure that your username is typed correctly. If you have repeated characters, it's easy to miss one of those characters as you type.

Did you add the @ symbol to your username? That symbol is used only to tag people in a comment in Instagram. So ditch the @ when you type your username.

If you still can't add your username, someone else may have changed your username. When you change your username or any other account information, you get an email message from Instagram informing you that your information was changed.

If you didn't get one in your email inbox or in your junk email folder, ask one of your friends or colleagues to log into Instagram, look at your profile, and find out if the username was changed. If your friend or colleague knows how to take a screenshot, have that person take a screenshot to send to you. After you review it, you can send it to Instagram if needed.

TIP

Do you suspect that your account was hacked? Instagram has suggestions for getting more help to secure your account at `https://help.instagram.com/149494825257596`. This page also contains a link to contact Instagram and explain what's happening.

Fixing password issues

If you've forgotten your Instagram account password, here are some suggestions for finding it. Or, as a last resort, resetting it so that you can get back to scratching your Instagram itch.

REMEMBER

If you're using your Facebook username and password to log in to Instagram, you'll have to open Facebook reset your password.

Checking your password

If you use a password manager app, open it to see your username or password in Instagram or Facebook. If you're using your Facebook account to log in to Instagram, you may want to log in to Facebook (or log out and log back in) to find out if your Facebook password is working properly.

Password management apps can become cranky from time to time and not work properly, so if you find that your Facebook or Instagram password doesn't work when you type it, you have several options to fix the problem:

>> Restart the password management app.

>> Restart your computer, smartphone, or tablet, and then try logging back into Instagram to see whether the password management app works properly.

>> Uninstall and reinstall the management app. Before you do this, write down all your accounts, usernames, and passwords . . . in a secure location, of course.

Finding your saved Instagram signup message

When you sign up or change your account information, you receive an email message that contains a link to log into your account as well as the email address you used to log in. Be sure to click the link in the email message so you can log in with the email address Instagram expects you to use. (The link includes your password so you don't have to enter it.)

REMEMBER

If you don't see the Instagram email in your inbox, check your junk email folder. If you find the message, you can tell your email app that messages from Instagram are not junk.

Resetting your password by email

If you don't have the email message you received from Instagram and you can't remember the password (or can't find it the password management app), you can reset your password. Simply follow these steps:

1. **Open the Instagram app, and then tap the Get Help Signing In link.**

The screen shown in Figure 15-4 (iOS users) or Figure 15-5 (Android users) appears.

2. **Tap Username or Email (iOS) or Use Username or Email (Android), and then type your Instagram username or email address.**

3. **Tap Send Login Link (iOS) or the send icon (Android), which is shown in the margin.**

You'll receive an email from Instagram in a few minutes.

If you mistyped your email address when you signed up for your account, you won't receive an email message in your inbox. In this case, reset your account information using the phone message detailed in the next step.

REMEMBER

FIGURE 15-4:
Getting password help on an iPhone.

FIGURE 15-5:
Getting help on an Android smartphone.

4. **Click or tap the Reset Your Instagram Password link in the email.**

The Instagram New Password web page appears in your browser.

5. **Type your new password.**

Resetting your password from your smartphone or tablet

If you don't have access to your email account, Instagram can send you a message on your smartphone or tablet (provided your tablet has a data plan). Here's how:

1. **Open the Instagram app, and then tap the Get Help Signing In link.**

iOS users see the Trouble Logging In? screen (refer to Figure 15-4). Android users see the Log In Help screen (refer to Figure 15-5).

2. **Tap Phone (iOS) or Send an SMS (Android) and then type your phone number.**

3. **Tap Send Login Link (iOS) or the send icon (Android), which is shown in the margin.**

   Your login link appears in a text message on your phone.

4. **Tap the login link in the text message.**

5. **Type your new password.**

WARNING

The link in the password reset email or text messages expires, though Instagram doesn't say when. If nothing happens when you tap the link in the message, you'll need to send another password reset email or text message.

Dealing with a disabled account

Instagram won't tell you that your account has been disabled for violation of its Community Guidelines until you try to log in and you see a message telling you that your account is disabled.

Now what? Enter your username and password, and then follow the onscreen instructions to try to appeal the decision. There are no guarantees that your account will be reinstated.

Finding Relief for Common Problems

If you run into problems uploading photos or videos, sharing with other Instagram users, or receiving notifications, read on to get some suggestions for finding solutions fast (and what to do if you can't).

Instagram won't share

Instagram has noted that problems exist when sharing your photos and videos with Facebook and Tumblr. You may encounter problems sharing your Instagram posts on Twitter, too.

TIP

If you want to learn about other sharing options, including copying a link so you can paste it into another social networking website, see Chapter 6.

You may have problems sharing your Instagram posts on Facebook, Twitter, or Tumblr for the simple reason that your preferred social network is down. In that case, you just have to wait until it fixes the problem.

If you verify on another smartphone, tablet, or computer that Facebook, Twitter, or Tumblr is operating normally, the link between Instagram and Facebook might have become disconnected. You can reset the link from a smartphone or tablet app by following the instructions in this section.

REMEMBER

If you still can't connect after you reset your links, the Instagram or Facebook app may have become corrupted. In that case, it's best to remove both apps and then reinstall them. Facebook and Instagram save your data, so you won't have to log in to both apps after you reinstall them.

Here's how to reset your linked Facebook, Twitter, or Tumblr accounts:

1. **Tap the Profile icon in the lower-right corner of the screen.**

The screen shown in Figure 15-6 (iOS) or Figure 15-7 (Android) appears.

FIGURE 15-6:
The Profile screen on an iPhone.

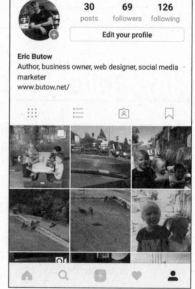

FIGURE 15-7:
The Profile screen on an Android smartphone.

2. **iOS users should tap the gear icon. Android users should tap the three dots icon.**

   Both icons are shown in the margin.

3. **Swipe up and tap Linked Accounts.**

   The Share Settings screen appears.

4. **Tap Facebook, Twitter, or Tumblr.**

5. **Tap Unlink Account.**

6. **Tap Yes, I'm Sure in the pop-up window that appears in the center of the screen.**

   Instagram and the other app (Facebook, Twitter, or Tumblr) are now unlinked.

7. **Tap Facebook, Twitter, or Tumblr.**

   This step reconnects the accounts. Try sharing your Instagram post again.

Getting Instagram to notify you

If you turned on notifications in the Instagram app but don't see notifications on your smartphone or tablet, check whether the Instagram app is sending you notifications.

Checking notifications on your iPhone or iPad

Here's how to check and set your Instagram notifications on your iPhone or iPad:

1. **On the home screen, tap Settings, and then tap Notifications.**

   The Notifications screen appears.

2. **In the apps list, swipe up and tap Instagram.**

3. **If the Allow Notifications entry is off, slide the switch from left to right.**

   If the slider is green and the switch is to the right side, notifications are on.

By default, Instagram notifications appear in Notification Center and on the Lock screen. You'll also see a Badge App icon and hear a sound when you receive an Instagram notification.

Checking notifications on your Android smartphone or tablet

Here's how to check and set Instagram notifications on your Android smartphone or tablet:

1. **On the home screen, tap Apps, then Settings, and then Applications.**

   The Applications screen appears.

2. **In the apps list, swipe up and tap Instagram.**

3. **Swipe up the Application Info screen until you see the Notifications option in the list.**

   If notifications are on, you'll see the word *Allowed* below the Notifications option. If they're off, the word *Blocked* appears.

4. **If notifications are off, tap the Notifications option and then turn on notifications.**

   You can also instruct Instagram to show notifications silently and make notifications a priority. When notifications are a priority, the notification will sound and turn on the screen when the Do Not Disturb feature is on.

Nothing Is Working . . . Now What?

When all else fails, you need to contact Instagram to report the problem. Instagram will need the following information to help you:

>> The type of smartphone or tablet you're using

>> The operating system and version you're using on your smartphone or tablet

>> When the problem occurs and how often it occurs

You can report a problem in the Instagram app on your iPhone, iPad, Android smartphone, or Android tablet.

Reporting a problem on your iPhone or iPad

If you are using Instagram on an iPhone or iPad, follow these steps to report a problem:

1. **Tap the Profile icon.**

2. **Tap the gear icon (shown in the margin).**

3. **Swipe up and tap Report a Problem.**

   The Report a Problem window appears.

4. **Tap Something Isn't Working.**

   The Feedback screen appears.

5. **Write your report.**

6. **Tap Send, in the upper-right corner.**

Reporting a problem on your Android smartphone or tablet

Here's how to report a problem if you own an Android smartphone or tablet.

1. **Tap the Profile icon.**

2. **Tap the three dots icon (shown in the margin).**

3. **Swipe up and tap Report a Problem.**

   The Report a Problem window appears.

4. **Tap Report a Problem.**

5. **Select the feature you're having a problem with, and then tap the next icon (right-pointing arrow), in the upper-right corner of the screen.**

   The Report a Problem screen appears.

6. **Write your report.**

7. **Tap the send icon (shown in the margin).**

Getting Rid of Error Messages

As with any app, you'll occasionally get error messages in the Instagram app on your iPhone, iPad, or Android device. And like any app, you may not understand why you're getting those error messages. In this section, we list four common error messages and how you can get around them.

Can't add a comment

If you receive an error message that states that you can't add a comment, one of these reasons may apply:

>> You can't include more than five tags in a comment. (You tag other Instagram users by typing the @ symbol before the username.)

>> You can add no more than 30 hashtags in a comment.

>> You can't post the same comment multiple times in one post.

>> Instagram filters out certain words and phrases, such as profanity, to meet its Community Guidelines.

>> You haven't updated Instagram recently to ensure that you have the most recent version.

If none of these reasons applies to you, close and restart the Instagram app. The next step is to turn your smartphone or tablet off and on, and then launch the Instagram app. Still not working? You need to contact Instagram for support, as described in the preceding section.

Can't delete comments

As of this writing, Instagram has a problem telling its users that a comment has been deleted. This problem arises if you try to delete a comment and get an error message that says the comment can't be deleted.

One potential solution is to close the Instagram app, restart it, and then view your post on the screen to see whether the comment is still there. If it is, you can close the Instagram app and clear all Instagram data as described earlier in the "Checking your space" section. That should clear out the deleted comment from your post.

If the comment is still there and you still get the error message when you try to delete the comment, your best option is to ignore it. By the time you read this, we hope that the problem will have been fixed or at least hidden effectively.

REMEMBER

You can delete only comments you've posted and comments from others about your posts.

Can't refresh feed

When you refresh your feed screen by swiping down, sometimes you won't see new posts. That could simply mean none of your followers have posted anything recently. However, if you can't refresh your feed over a period of time, it could be due to one of the following:

>> Your Wi-Fi signal is weak, or you're in an area with heavy Wi-Fi network usage, thus weakening the connection.

>> You've reached the limits of your carrier's data plan. You'll need to find a Wi-Fi network or shell out money for more data in your plan.

>> Instagram is having some issues. You'll just have to be patient.

If all else fails, report the problem in the Instagram app as described in the preceding section, and see whether Instagram can figure out what's wrong with the app.

Can't follow anyone else

If you receive a message that says you can't follow anyone else, check your profile to see how many other Instagram users you're following. If it's 7,500, you won't be able to add any other followers.

Most people will never reach the 7,500 limit. If you receive this error message and you are below (even well below) the limit, report the problem in the Instagram app so you can work with Instagram support to solve the mystery.

REMEMBER

There is no limit to the number of Instagram users who can follow you.

WARNING

Instagram has an unadvertised limit to the number of people you can follow per hour and per day. The maximum amount of Instagram users you can follow is 20 per hour and 480 followers per day. If you reach this limit, you'll have to wait until the top of the next hour or the beginning of the next day to follow someone.

Chapter **16**

Insta-Help Is on the Way

I f you ever need help using Instagram, plenty of online resources are available to supplement this book. In addition, the app itself contains online help that you can refer to quickly.

What's more, if you can't run the Instagram app, you can find help on the Instagram website, on Instagram social media profiles, and on other social-networking and community websites.

In this chapter, you start by learning about Instagram's online help in the app as well as on the Instagram website. Then you find out how to contact Instagram through its social media profiles as well as the Instagram blog. Finally, see how to join an online community so you can get help from other Instagram users.

Taking Advantage of Instagram's Help

Help Center, shown in Figure 16-1, should be the first place you look for a solution to your problem. To access Help Center on the Instagram website, go to https://help.instagram.com/.

FIGURE 16-1:
Instagram Help
Center on a
desktop browser.

Accessing Help Center

If the Instagram app is installed on a iPhone, iPad, or an Android smartphone or tablet, and the app isn't working, you can access Help Center not only on the website but also on the Windows Instagram app if that app is installed. If your smartphone or tablet app is working, you can also access Help Center from the app at any time.

On the iPhone or iPad

Here's how to view the Help Center screen if you are using an iPhone or an iPad:

1. **Tap the Profile icon, in the lower-right corner of the screen.**

2. **Tap the gear icon, shown in the margin.**

   The Options screen appears.

3. **Swipe up and tap Help Center.**

The Help Center screen shown in Figure 16-2 appears.

Swipe to view all the topics. Tap a topic title to view more information about that topic.

When you're finished viewing information in Help Center, return to the Options screen by tapping the < icon, in the upper-left corner.

On an Android smartphone or tablet

You view Help Center in your web browser on your Android smartphone or tablet. Here's how:

1. **Tap the Profile icon, in the lower-right corner of the screen.**

2. **Tap the three dots icon (menu), shown in the margin.**

   The Options screen appears.

3. **Swipe up and tap Instagram Help Center.**

   The Open With window appears.

    REMEMBER

   If you already selected your default browser app in Instagram or another app, the Help Center web page will appear in your default browser automatically.

4. **Tap Chrome to open the Help Center web page in Google Chrome, or tap Samsung Internet to view the web page in the Samsung Internet app.**

5. **If you see the Default App Selected window in the center of the screen, tap OK.**

Now you see the Help Center screen in your browser app, as shown in Figure 16-3.

FIGURE 16-2:
Swipe to view all options in Help Center.

(Figure shows an Instagram Help Center screen with the following visible text:)

●○○○○ AT&T 🗢 3:44 PM @ ✈ ✻ 100% ▭✦

Instagram

Q Ask a question

- Using Instagram
- Managing Your Account
- Login & Troubleshooting
- Privacy & Safety
- Instagram for Business

What's New

- Keeping Instagram Safe
- Sharing Posts with Multiple Photos and Videos
- Archiving and Updating the @WhiteHouse Account
- Adding Stickers to Your Story

Swipe in the screen to view all the topics. Tap a topic title to view more information about that topic.

When you've finished viewing information in Help Center, return to the Options screen in the Instagram app by opening the Recent Apps screen and then either closing your browser window or tapping the Instagram tile if you plan to return to the Help Center later. (The steps for opening the Recent Apps screen depend on the device, so we can't list them here.)

In the Windows app

After you open the Windows Instagram app, here's how to get to Help Center:

1. **Click the Profile icon, in the lower-right corner of the window.**

2. **Click the gear icon, shown in the margin.**

   The Profile screen appears.

3. **In the list on the left, scroll down and click Help Center.**

   Help Center appears in the right pane, as shown in Figure 16-4.

Click a topic title on the left side of the pane to view more information about that topic.

When you've finished viewing information in Help Center, return to the Profile screen by clicking the < icon, in the upper-left corner.

FIGURE 16-3:
Help Center on an Android device.

Visiting Privacy and Safety Center

Review Instagram's Privacy and Safety Center so you know how to use Instagram wisely and what to do if you think someone is using Instagram in the wrong way (which may or may not be affecting you directly).

FIGURE 16-4:
Help Center in the Windows app.

In the Help Center screen, open Privacy and Safety Center by selecting Privacy and Safety. A list of topics appears, as shown in Figure 16-5.

Viewing Instagram Business web pages

The Instagram website has a dedicated business website that you can access at https://business.instagram.com. The website, shown in Figure 16-6, contains information on setting up a new business account, promoting your posts, learning how to get the most from your business account, and more.

If you can't access the Instagram Business website or you prefer to work with the mother ship (Facebook), visit the Facebook Business website at www.facebook.com/business/help/976240832426180.

FIGURE 16-5:
Privacy and Safety topics on an iPhone.

The Facebook Business website contains much of the same information as the Instagram Business website, including details on advertising on Instagram, targeting ads for the best results, and Instagram Business Tools. You may want to look at both the Instagram Business and Facebook Business websites to ensure that you get the most complete information about promoting your business in Instagram effectively.

Tapping Social Media

Instagram doesn't keep its communications limited to Instagram. It maintains close connections with Facebook and its Facebook Business website (two billion profiles and counting as of this writing).

Instagram also posts regularly on its Twitter profile, which is no surprise because you can share your posts directly on Twitter from the Instagram app.

What's more, Instagram's blogs for both personal and business users can help you learn more about using Instagram and become inspired to create a post or two.

Sending a message on Facebook

Instagram for Business has a Facebook profile at www.facebook.com/
instagramforbusiness, shown in Figure 16-7.

FIGURE 16-7:
The Instagram for
Business page on
Facebook.

You can view posts from Instagram by scrolling down or swiping up. You can
access the Instagram Business website by clicking or tapping the Learn More
button. As of this writing, you can even call the number on the Instagram for
Business Facebook page.

Tweeting and being tweeted

The Instagram Twitter feed, at https://twitter.com/instagram, gives you the
latest information. You can also find photos, videos, and links to Instagram posts
that Instagram thinks are interesting, as shown in Figure 16-8.

Scroll in your web browser or swipe in the Twitter app screen to view recent posts.
Click or tap links to view the Instagram post or linked article.

FIGURE 16-8:
Follow the
Instagram feed
by clicking or
tapping the
Follow button in
the upper right.

On the left side of the screen, you can click or tap links to get help with Instagram, read the Instagram blog, and send a tweet to Instagram. There's no telling if Instagram will respond, but you never know until you try . . . er, tweet.

Reading the Instagram blog

Speaking of the Instagram blog, you can view the general Instagram blog at `http://blog.instagram.com` on your web browser. You can also access the blog from one of your Instagram apps instead.

On the iPhone or iPad

Here's how to view the Instagram blog on an iPhone or iPad:

1. **Tap the Profile icon, in the lower-right corner of the screen.**

2. **Tap the gear icon, shown in the margin.**

   The Options screen appears.

3. **Swipe up and tap Blog.**

   The latest blog post summary appears in your browser app (see Figure 16-9).

Swipe in the Blog screen to view all post summaries. Tap a post summary title to read the entire post in the Post screen.

After you've read a post, return to the Blog screen by tapping <, near the top center of the screen. Return to the Options screen from the Blog or Post screen by tapping <, in the upper-left corner.

On an Android smartphone or tablet

On an Android smartphone or tablet, you can view Instagram the blog in your web browser. Here's how:

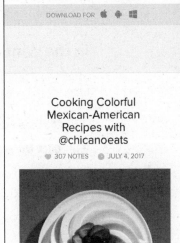

FIGURE 16-9:
The Instagram blog within the Instagram app on the iPhone or iPad.

1. **Tap the Profile icon, in the lower-right corner of the screen.**

2. **Tap the three dots icon (menu), shown in the margin.**

   The Options screen appears.

3. **Swipe up and tap Blog.**

   The Open With window appears.

   If you already selected your default browser app in Instagram or another app, the Blog web page will appear in your default browser automatically.

REMEMBER

4. **Tap Chrome to open the Help Center web page in Google Chrome, or tap Samsung Internet to view the web page in the Samsung Internet app.**

5. **If you see the Default App Selected window in the center of the screen, tap OK.**

Now you see the Instagram Blog page in your browser. Swipe in the screen to view blog post summaries. Tap a topic title to view more information about that topic.

When you've finished viewing the Instagram blog, return to the Options screen in the Instagram app by opening the Recent Apps screen and then either closing your browser window or tapping the Instagram tile if you plan to return to the Help

Center later. (The steps for opening the Recent Apps screen depend on the device, so we can't list them here.)

TIP

If you have the Tumblr app, you can open the blog in Tumblr by tapping Open in App, at the top of the screen. (If you don't have Tumblr installed, you can get the app from the Google Play Store by tapping Get the Tumblr App, at the bottom of the screen.)

In the Windows app

After you open the Windows Instagram app, here's how to get to the Instagram blog:

1. **Click the Profile icon, in the lower-right corner.**

2. **Click the gear icon, shown in the margin.**

   The Profile screen appears.

3. **In the list on the left, scroll down and click Blog.**

   The Instagram Blog page appears in the right pane.

Scroll up and down in the screen to view blog post summaries. Click on a topic title to view more information about that topic.

Once you've read the post, return to the Instagram Blog page by clicking the < icon, above the blog post. You can return to the Profile screen either from the Blog or Post screen by clicking the < icon, in the upper-left corner of the screen.

Visiting the Instagram Business blog

Instagram Business also has a separate blog, but you can't get to it from your Instagram app. Instead, you need to go to your web browser and type `https://business.instagram.com/blog/`. Or go to the Instagram Business website at `https://business.instagram.com` and tap the Blog link, in the upper-right corner.

The blog appears, as shown in Figure 16-10. Swipe or scroll to view recent post summaries. To read a post, tap the summary title, photo, or description.

FIGURE 16-10:
The Instagram
Business blog.

Joining a Community

Instagram makes it easy for you to join communities — and not just the ones on its Facebook and Twitter feeds. You can join or start an InstaMeet, which is a great way to network in person with other Instagram users to take photos, shoot videos, and talk about Instagram.

What if you don't want to start an InstaMeet, but you're not getting answers to your questions? Scan Reddit and Topix, two popular discussion websites, to find an interesting discussion — or start one of your own.

Joining other Instagrammers in an InstaMeet

If you want to join an InstaMeet, you have to access the Instagram Community website at `https://community.instagram.com`. Sorry, but you can't access the Community website through the Instagram app.

If you want to find an InstaMeet near you, swipe or scroll until you see a map indicating where InstaMeets are happening near you (see Figure 16-11). You can zoom in the map for more detailed information.

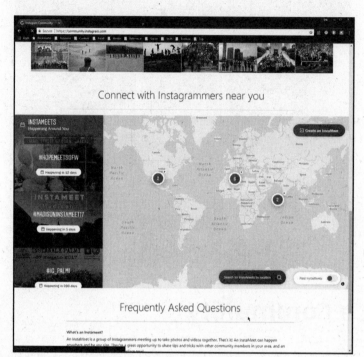

FIGURE 16-11: Tap the number in the map to view InstaMeets in that area.

Starting an InstaMeet

If you don't find an InstaMeet near you and want to start your own, swipe or scroll until you see the Host Your Own section, shown in Figure 16-12. The InstaMeet Inspiration section below Host Your Own will give you a few guidelines for creating an InstaMeet. For inspiration, tap or click the Instagram Blog link (refer to the bottom of Figure 16-12).

Tell Instagram about your InstaMeet when it's over by swiping or scrolling to the bottom of the page and then selecting the Tell Us about It link and filling out the online form.

TIP

If you work in a business with at least a few employees and they're interested in Instagram, consider running an InstaMeet with your co-workers (and maybe a boss or two). Then you can see how successful the event is, post photos and videos about the experience for your followers, and use that publicity and experience to generate interest in an InstaMeet for your customers.

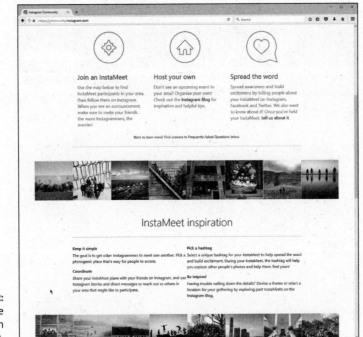

Visiting Reddit and Topix

You can also join online communities to talk about Instagram. Two of the most popular (and busy) websites are Reddit and Topix.

WARNING

Some of the messages you'll find on these online communities are inappropriate or even NSFW (Not Suitable For Work). If you're going to search for messages in these online communities, you may want to ensure that no one else can see your screen before you start reading.

Reddit

Visit the Reddit Instagram page at www.reddit.com/r/Instagram/ (see Figure 16-13). Swipe or scroll to view the list of messages. If comments are included with the message, you'll see the number of comments below the message title.

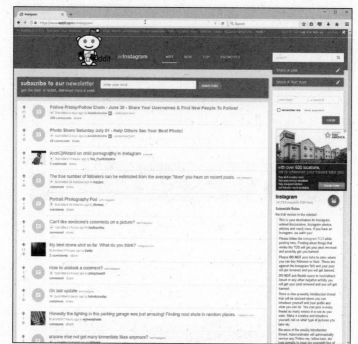

FIGURE 16-13:
The Reddit
Instagram page.

You can also search for messages with one or more specific search terms. Here's how:

1. **In the Search box in the upper-right corner of the web page, type your term(s).**

2. **Tap or click the Limit My Search to r/Instagram check box.**

   Selecting the check box will ensure that you don't get results from all Reddit forums that match your term(s).

3. **Tap or click the magnifying glass icon on the right side of the Search box.**

   A list of posts with titles that contain your search term(s) appears on the page. Scroll or swipe up and down to view all the posts.

When you find a post you want to read more about, tap or click the post title to open it. You can leave a comment as well as share the message on your Facebook, Twitter, or Tumblr account.

Topix

Topix also has its own Instagram page at www.topix.com/forum/iphone-apps/ instagram. Swipe or scroll to view the list of recent messages, as shown in Figure 16-14. Tap or click Next to go to the next page in the message list.

The number of comments appears to the right of the message title in the list. Note, though, that the original message counts as one comment.

You can search all messages for one or more terms by tapping or clicking in the Search This Forum box at the top of the page, typing your search term(s), and then tapping or clicking the orange magnifying glass to the right of the box. A new web page with a list of all message topics that contain your search term(s) appears.

Tap or click the message title to read the original message and any comments. To reply to a message or comment, tap or click Reply below the message or comment. Return to the list of messages by tapping or clicking your browser's back button.

TIP

You can write your own message for other users to read and comment on by tapping the orange Start Discussion box above the list.

6 The Part of Tens

Find companies and individual Instagram users getting their creative on.

Look to your competitors' Instagram accounts for ideas for your business profile.

» Sugarandcloth, RPMItalian

» EmilyJoyRosen, TheLoveBombCo

» The.Book.Report, LaJollaMom

» TSA, GeneralElectric

Chapter **17**

Ten Brands Killing It on Instagram

t's so easy to tell you what to do; it's a lot harder to do those things. That's why it helps to see what other great Instagram brands are doing and use them for inspiration.

Throughout the book, we talk about Instagram tactics and best practices. Now we want to show you ten accounts that are great examples of these recommendations.

GoPro

For a big brand, @GoPro understands the effect of using Instagram well. GoPro's content is a mix of people, places, and pets. Although its photos and videos span every corner of the globe, they are cohesive, well branded, and share the same story of adventure and excitement. Figure 17-1 gives an example of the posts shared on the GoPro account.

The most unique aspect of the GoPro account is that its content is all user-generated content (UGC). Its posts are photos and videos created by its customers, which it *regrams* (repost) to its account. GoPro chooses only the best content and posts that stay true to its brand's styling and personality.

Beyond the branding, GoPro also does a good job of interacting with its audience, posting fun captions and responding to comments and questions on its posts. GoPro builds engagement and loyalty through this method of communication.

Yellowillow

The @yellowillow Instagram account, run by photographer Anne McIsaac, has beautiful styling in which most of her images incorporate the color yellow, as shown in Figure 17-2. She shares images from her work and life, in a range of topics and locations, but are all tied together with her photographic style and the pops of yellow color.

Anne incorporates effective hashtag strategies as well as a brief description or story about the post, giving it context and personality. She is also dedicated to her audience, responding to comments and questions to build a relationship with her followers.

Thanks to the size of her audience and the value she has as a brand, Anne collaborates with other companies to create sponsored posts. Even though these posts are promoting another product or company, she ensures that the content stays true to her own branding and personality.

FIGURE 17-1:
GoPro shares great well-branded content.

FIGURE 17-2:
The @yellowillow account incorporates yellow into post content.

Sugarandcloth

Ashley Rose is a blogger who uses her @sugarandcloth Instagram account to build her brand. Her Instagram posts are a combination of her lifestyle, blog projects, and insights into her many projects. Her images are colorful and vibrant, making them visually appealing to users on Instagram.

She also writes great captions that showcase her personality and style, allowing her to connect authentically with her audience. Figure 17-3 provides a sampling of the beautiful images on the @sugarandcloth account.

Beyond her regular Instagram content, Ashley uses Instagram Stories effectively as well. Her Stories are consistent with her branding and styling but open up her life as a mom, wife, blogger, and business owner. She shares the more personal side of her business and allows her personality to shine through.

FIGURE 17-3:
The @sugarandcloth account uses bright, vibrant colors.

RPMItalian

RPM Italian is a restaurant in Chicago, Illinois, that showcases its cuisine, restaurant, and news via its @rpmitalian Instagram account. Every photo has great staging and lighting. RPM Italian effectively incorporates behind-the-scenes content, such as making pasta from scratch or showcasing chefs in the kitchen, while editing and staging the photos to align with its brand styling of plated dishes.

Black and white is the dominant undertone of the images, yet pops of color add visual appeal. Figure 17-4 shows you how RPM Italian achieves this brand styling on Instagram.

FIGURE 17-4:
The @rpmitalian account shares a variety of images from its restaurant.

This account also shares posts on a minimal schedule, at most two to three times a week. In this way, it ensures that its content is of the highest quality and has the greatest effect on its audience.

EmilyJoyRosen

Emily Joy Rosen, the CEO of the Institute for the Psychology of Eating, uses her @emilyjoyrosen Instagram account as a micro-blog. Although it's generally advised to keep captions to no more than a few short paragraphs on Instagram, Emily is an example of the exception to the rule, as shown in Figure 17-5.

All her posts have long captions, broken up by spacing and formatting, to tell a moving story. Emily connects with her audience through raw, emotional details of her own life. And even though most people don't like to read long captions on Instagram, her audience appreciates her approach and happily reads each post.

Adding to the relationship building on her account, Emily actively engages with her audience in the comments of each post. She offers support and encouragement to those who need it.

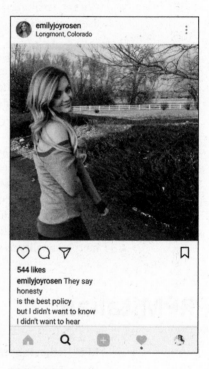

FIGURE 17-5:
The @emilyjoyrosen account uses long captions to connect emotionally with her audience.

TheLoveBombCo

The Love Bomb Company sells coffee mugs and glassware imprinted with witty motivational sayings. Its @thelovebombco Instagram account is a direct representation of its brand, voice, and style. When you view this account — from the bio to posts and products — you immediately get a sense of what this company is about (whether you love it or hate it), as shown in Figure 17-6.

This company understands that always posting its products can get overwhelming and appear pushy. So instead of only showcasing its products, it includes quotes in branded fonts.

It also connects more authentically with its audience by including user-generated content provided by its customers. This highlights its products in various settings and shows the variety of lifestyles, yet commonalities, of its customers.

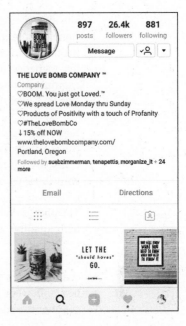

The.Book.Report

The @the.book.report account on Instagram makes great use of videos and multi-image posts (also called albums or slide shows), two effective but underutilized Instagram features. Michelle, who runs the Instagram account, provides reviews of children's books and uses her Instagram account to share her opinions as well as a look at each book.

She uses the slide show post to share an image of the book cover, as shown in Figure 17-7, and then a series of images or a video to showcase the inside of the book. Her captions contain her insights into the book and its value to other parents.

To create trust and rapport with her audience, Michelle also incorporates posts about her family and kids, demonstrating their personal life and interests.

LaJollaMom

The @lajollamom account is run by Katie Dillon, a luxury travel blogger. Her account is full of beautiful photos from around the world, but

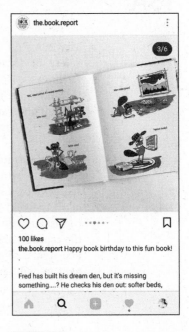

FIGURE 17-7:
The @the.book.report account uses a variety of features to provide book reviews.

she also does a fantastic job of sharing educational content. Her captions often include insider tips, fun facts, or other information that her audience finds valuable. Figure 17-8 is an example of one of her post captions providing tips on traveling.

Katie often shares personal experiences of her travels with her family as well. It provides transparency to her audience and builds trust with those who follow her.

The photos on her account are personalized but high-quality images that are edited and selected for best performance on Instagram. As with most of the other examples in this chapter, Katie ensures that she interacts with her followers by personally responding to comments and questions on her posts.

TSA

The TSA — the agency that ensures traveler safety at airports and other transportation facilities — isn't an account you would expect to follow on Instagram. However, the @TSA account understands how to do Instagram well, as shown in Figure 17-9.

It showcases its working dogs and handlers on Instagram, which helps because people love to see dogs on Instagram! It also shares photos of all the wild and crazy items that have been confiscated by TSA agents. In these posts, the captions are used to remind you of prohibited items, so there's an educational component in addition to the humor behind the odd objects.

Liked by **anntranfashion** and **656 others**
lajollamom Reflections on summer in Beijing. It rained when we were at Temple of Heaven park which surrounds the religious buildings. Emperors from the Ming and Qing dynasties used to come here to pray for a good harvest. The rain tempered the scorching temps so we were grateful for whomever asked for it. ;)

My advice... Come to this park with plenty of time to spare (or a guide) as it's very easy to get lost here despite the maps. But it's gorgeous and almost hard to believe it's in the middle of an enormous city. Have

FIGURE 17-8:
The @lajollamom account uses captions to educate and inform Katie's audience.

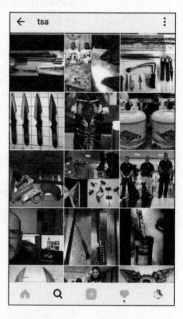

FIGURE 17-9:
The @TSA Instagram account is full of items people have attempted to pass through security.

To keep its account more lighthearted, the @TSA account will often get involved in trending topics or relevant events, such as the solar eclipse or Star Wars Day.

GeneralElectric

For a large engineering company, focused on business-to-business customers, the @generalelectric Instagram account does a surprisingly good job. This account doesn't attempt to focus on large-scale clients. Instead, it builds brand awareness and connects with people on an individual level.

This Instagram account incorporates employee profiles, inside looks at product development, tours of the company's facilities, and information about how things are built. Its posts are informational and educational, yet entertaining to view or read. Figure 17-10 is an example of a fun and informational post about the design of its wind turbines.

This account also effectively incorporates photos, videos, and slide show posts to best generate engagement with a wide range of its audience.

FIGURE 17-10:
The @generalelectric account shares fun and educational content to build brand awareness.

Chapter 18

Ten Places to Find Inspiration

The tactics and methods for using Instagram for your business are often methodical. But what really connects with people and your audience is good content. Posts that evoke emotions or educate your viewers will always perform well for you.

If you're unsure of where to start or what types of content you want to create, look for inspiration from others on Instagram. Seeing what they are doing can give you the ideas and motivation to create unique and valuable content of your own.

In this chapter, we show you ten great sources of inspiration on Instagram.

Investigate the Explore Page

One of the first places to look for inspiration on Instagram is the Explore page, shown in Figure 18-1.

To get to the Explore page:

>> On your mobile device: Tap the magnifying glass icon in the Instagram toolbar.

>> On the Windows app and the desktop version of the Instagram website: Click the compass icon at the top of the screen (to the left of the heart icon).

The Explore page curates posts from a variety of Instagram users. The content is found and sorted specifically for you, based on the types of accounts you follow and interact with. What you see on the Explore page will always be different than what others will see, because each user receives customized results.

TIP

You can easily refresh the Explore page to see new content by swiping down on the screen on your mobile device.

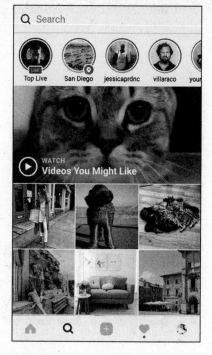

FIGURE 18-1:
The Explore page displays a variety of content that is targeted toward your interests.

This page includes Stories along the top (in circles) and a combination of videos and photos that might interest you. You can tap any post to view it in its entirety, including the caption and comments.

The content on the Explore page is valuable as a source of inspiration because most of the posts are from people you don't currently follow, so you're introduced to new accounts and fresh content. And that content is usually high performing (photos and videos that generate a lot of engagement compared to their account follower size), so you'll see the type of content that generates positive reactions.

Review Hashtag Searches Related to Your Brand

Hashtags are a popular way to find content centered on a specific theme or phrase. There's no reason you shouldn't be using this same resource to find inspiration!

You can perform a hashtag search on Instagram in two ways. The first is to tap any hashtag you see in an Instagram post. The corresponding hashtag gallery in Instagram appears, as shown in Figure 18-2, and you see all recent content created using the hashtag you tapped.

The second method for accessing hashtag searches follows:

1. **On the Instagram page, tap the magnifying glass.**

   The Explore page appears.

2. **In the Search field at the top, type the hashtag option you want to search for.**

   To follow along with the example, type **#photography**.

3. **Tap the Tags tab.**

   The Tags screen shows results from the hashtag you entered, plus any related hashtags.

   Figure 18-3 shows the results of our search for #photography. As you can see, related hashtags that start with *photography* also appear in the list.

   TIP

   Using this search function with a keyword for your industry is a great way to find other related hashtags that you might want to use on your own content or search for more ideas.

4. **Tap a hashtag in the list to open up the corresponding hashtag gallery.**

Searching these hashtags, especially when searching topics and keywords related to your business or industry, is a resourceful way to find fresh content. And best of all, because the content is in line with what you're looking to create, you should be able to get some good ideas of what others in a similar industry are doing and pull inspiration from those posts.

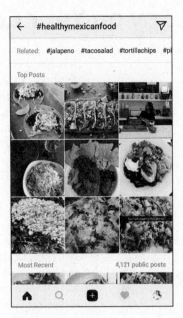

FIGURE 18-2:
A hashtag gallery displays the Instagram posts that include the hashtag you tapped.

FIGURE 18-3:
The hashtag search screen populates other hashtags with your related keyword.

Spy on Your Competitors

Nothing's wrong with a little healthy competition! In fact, it can make for great inspiration. You most likely already know who your competitors are in your business. Look them up on Instagram to see what they're doing and get ideas of what you may (or may not) want to emulate in some way for your content.

If you aren't following your competitors on Instagram, you may need to search for them. Just as you did with the hashtag searches, tap the magnifying glass icon on the home page to display the Explore page. Next, tap the Search field and start typing either the business name, if you know it, or a type of business or a physical location or both. Then tap the People tab to see all accounts that match that criteria, as shown in Figure 18-4. Tapping any name in the list will take you to that Instagram profile.

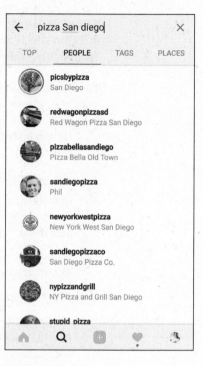

FIGURE 18-4:
Use the Search field and the People tab to look up your competitors.

Of course, you don't want to copy what your competitors are doing. But seeing how their content is created, how often they post, and what hashtags they use can give you some direction in your own strategy.

Even if your competitor posts content that you don't find appealing or that doesn't generate much engagement, that information is helpful to know. You can use it as inspiration for the types of content to avoid in your own strategy.

Get Inspiration from Local Businesses

Beyond looking at your direct competitors, it can be helpful to look at businesses in your local area. These accounts may be creating quality content that showcases your city or region. You may be able to draw inspiration from the local flare they utilize in their content. You may also be able to find some good local hashtags to use in your own posts based on what other local companies are using.

If your business is local or has one or more physical locations, consider incorporating content in your Instagram strategy that highlights local or regional attractions. For example, if you own a shoe store, including content related to your local parks, city walks, or even live events can be a great way to connect with your target audience. It reinforces that you are part of the community and reminds active people that they need good shoes.

Check Out Your Favorite Products

Many of the brands you already know and love are likely using Instagram as well. And if you already enjoy those products, chances are you'll like the content they're sharing on Instagram too. Check out those favorite products and companies on Instagram to get some fun inspiration for your own content.

Look for brands that are creating content regularly and that you find visually appealing. You might find creative ways to stage your products to make them more flattering or appealing.

Finding content that also showcases humor, education, or other entertainment value is also helpful. Figure 18-5 shows you three examples of products in which the companies got creative with their content to best appeal to their target audience.

FIGURE 18-5: Products with appealing Instagram posts.

From small and local companies to global brands, there are many brands using Instagram well and which can provide inspiration for your Instagram content.

Look to Photographers

Great photography performs the best on Instagram. Regardless of the value of your message, people will scroll right past your post if you use a poor-quality image. Improve your photography skills and find inspiration by following actual photographers on Instagram.

Good photographers have a sense of composition, alignment, and lighting that helps them create beautiful photographs. Finding photographers who appeal to your style can help you see the types of photo staging that will improve your own photography skills.

Depending on the types of objects you plan to showcase on Instagram, look for photographers with a similar subject. For example, Figure 18-6 shows you two photographers with a different focus, one on people and the other on objects and landscapes.

FIGURE 18-6: Photographers often focus on a specific type of photography.

Get Inspired by Bloggers

Many bloggers make good use of Instagram to build their audience and to motivate their audience to take action on the posts they're sharing. Whether encouraging viewers to, say, read something, follow a recipe, or fix up a DIY project, Instagram often helps these bloggers reach their goals.

Bloggers who create beautiful content and drive engagement and interactions are great sources of inspiration. Most of them have vibrant photos with beautiful finished projects. Seeing how these accounts create attractive content can help you determine how to stage and set up your own content to best appeal to your target audience.

Most bloggers also have cohesive galleries on Instagram. Even though all of their posts showcase a different item or project, they have a consistent style and theme. These posts should help inspire you to create your own style and theme to keep your content branded and cohesive. Figure 18-7 demonstrates two bloggers who do this well.

FIGURE 18-7: Bloggers often create cohesive galleries that appeal visually to their audience.

Find Big Brands That Are Being Creative

A lot of big brands get creative with their Instagram content and campaigns. Although they often have the advantage of large budgets and teams of creative input, you can take all their hard work as inspiration for your own content.

Take a look at big brands to see how they incorporate storytelling, employee profiles, company updates, or product launches. When you see how massive organizations are able to connect on a personal level with their audience, you can find similar ways to reach out to your audience.

Figure 18-8 provides three examples of large companies that connect in humorous and effective ways with their audiences.

FIGURE 18-8: Big brands get creative on Instagram.

You can find inspiration in how big brands not only connect with their audience but also take time to create a strong and timely message that resonates well.

Learn from Instagram and Marketing Experts

To stay on top of what is and is no longer working well on Instagram, we recommend that you follow industry leaders in Instagram and social media marketing. These accounts often post breaking news or Instagram tactics to help you better create an effective Instagram strategy. Because Instagram does release updates regularly, having a good resource for current news and tactics is beneficial.

Industry leaders often begin implementing new tactics and features quickly, so you can see them in use and can determine how to incorporate them in your own content strategy.

Some of the best resources for Instagram news and updates follow:

>> @jenns_trends

>> @coreycwalker

>> @smexaminer

>> @tylerjmccall

>> @suebzimmerman

>> @mollymarshallmarketing

Follow the Instagram for Business Account

As we just mentioned, Instagram is always updating the app and adding features. It also does a lot to highlight companies that use Instagram for marketing. Instagram has created @instagramforbusiness, shown in Figure 18-9, to help you better understand Instagram as a marketing tool.

To stay abreast of the latest features and updates, and grab inspiration from other businesses using Instagram marketing, follow the Instagram for Business account.

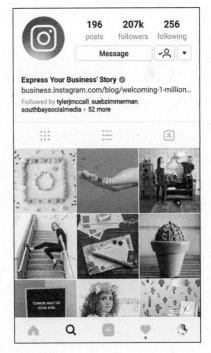

FIGURE 18-9:
The Instagram for Business account on Instagram.

Index

D

delete icon (X), 61, 93
deleting
  comments, 92–94, 236
  video, 72–73
demographics, 160
deselecting photos, 65
design
  advertising requirements, 164–165
  contest images, 196–197
determining
  brand voice, 37–38
  contest length, 195
  post content, 43
Dillon, Katie (travel blogger), 261–262
Direct Messages (DM)
  replying to, 86–87
  sending Instagram Stories using, 137–138
disabled accounts, 231
disabling filters, 55
displaying
  business web pages, 243–244
  followers, 106
  Insights via Facebook Ads Manager, 187–188
  Insights via Instagram, 185–186
DM (Direct Messages)
  replying to, 86–87
  sending Instagram Stories using, 137–138
drawing on Instagram Stories, 148–149

E

editing photos, 53–59, 67
editing tools, 55–58
emailing
  hashtags, 118
  resetting passwords by, 229–230
embedding
  Instagram feed on websites, 209–210
  photos/videos on web pages, 83–85
EmilyJoyRosen, 260
emojis, adding to bio, 28

engagement, contest, 198–199
entry requirements, for contests, 194
envisioning your look, 38–40
error messages, troubleshooting, 235–237
establishing entry requirements for contests, 194
evaluating third-party scheduling and analytics platforms, 46–48
event hashtag, 211, 212
events, 211–214
exclamation point, 92, 93
executing contests, 199–200
Explore function/page, 100–101, 265–266
exposure, changing, 67

F

face filters, 153–154
Facebook
  about, 218, 219
  connecting to pages, 32–33
  creating ads using, 173–183
  finding your friends from, 98–99
  logging in from, 16, 228
  sending messages on, 245
  sharing on, 61, 62, 231–232
Facebook Ads Manager, 162, 166, 172, 173, 174–178, 178–179, 187–188
Facebook Business Manager, 31, 243–244
Facebook Power Editor, 166, 172, 173, 179–183
Fade tool, 58
fans, alerting, 157
favorite products, 269–270
Federal Communications Commission (FCC), 191
Federal Trade Commission (FTC), 190–191
feeds, refreshing, 237
Filter screen, 53
filter thumbnail images (Filter screen), 53
filters
  adding, 55, 67
  applying, 53–54, 66–67, 74
  disabling, 55
  face, 153–154
  reordering, 54

About the Authors

Jenn Herman is a social media consultant, speaker, and globally recognized Instagram expert. She is the forefront blogger on Instagram marketing and her blog, Jenn's Trends, has won the title of a Top 10 Social Media Blog in 2014, 2015, and 2016. Through her blog, consulting, and speaking, Jenn provides tips, resources, and training for small to medium sized businesses that need to structure their social media strategies.

Jenn has been featured in Inc., Fox News, Yahoo! Finance, and numerous other podcasts and publications. She is the author of the self-published books *The Ultimate Beginner's Guide to Instagram* and *Stop Guessing: Your Step-by-Step Guide to Creating a Social Media Strategy*. Jenn's Instagram username is jenns_trends.

Eric Butow is the owner of Butow Communications Group (BCG) in Jackson, California. BCG offers online marketing analysis and improvement services for businesses of all sizes. He has written 30 computing and user experience books. His most recent books include *Google Glass For Dummies* (Wiley), *My Samsung Galaxy S7* (Que), and *Samsung Gear S2 For Dummies* (Wiley).

When he's not working in (and on) his business or writing books, you can find Eric enjoying time with his friends, walking around the historic Gold Rush town of Jackson, and helping his mother manage her infant and toddler daycare business. Eric's Instagram username is ericbutow.

Corey Walker is the owner of The Marketing Specialist in El Dorado Hills, California. The Marketing Specialist offers social media strategy, content, ad management and analytics with a concentrated passion for Instagram and Facebook. She has managed the social media accounts of hospitals, medical groups, real estate agents, online businesses, and publications.

When she's not online, you can find her and her husband cheering on her daughters at a volleyball tournament or a soccer game, or gathering with friends and neighbors for a night of good food and wine. Corey's Instagram username is coreycwalker.

Dedications

To my daughter, who motivates me to do so much more.
— Jenn Herman

To my family and friends.
— Eric Butow

To my husband and two lovely daughters.
— Corey Walker

Authors' Acknowledgments

I'd like to thank the team of people who made this book happen. My co-authors, Eric Butow and Corey Walker, made it a pleasure and I'm honored to have worked alongside them. My family and friends cheered me on and encouraged me through all the late-night writing sessions. My agent for this book, Carole Jelen, held my hand through the process. And the team at Wiley, including editors Amy Fandrei and Susan Pink, made us look good! Finally, thanks to you and every other business owner or marketer who wants to learn how to use Instagram effectively and is willing to invest in that commitment.
— Jenn Herman

I'd like to thank my co-authors, Jenn Herman and Corey Walker, for being such wonderful people to work with. My thanks as always to Carole Jelen— I'm lucky to have her as my literary agent. I also want to thank all the pros at Wiley who made this book possible, especially acquisitions editor Amy Fandrei and project editor Susan Pink. And I also thank you for buying this book.
— Eric Butow

So many people helped me in this book-writing journey. First and foremost, it was a wonderful collaboration working with my co-authors, Jenn Herman and Eric Butow. My family was very supportive and gave me the time I needed to write, even when it meant writing all weekend. Our literary agent, Carole Jelen, was a huge help in getting this book underway, and Wiley acquisitions editor Amy Fandrei and editor Susan Pink smoothed out all our writing kinks! I also want to thank my friends and extended family, who inquired regularly about the book's progress, and all future Instagram pros who purchase this book.
— Corey Walker

Publisher's Acknowledgments

Acquisitions Editor: Amy Fandrei

Project Editor: Susan Pink

Copy Editor: Susan Pink

Technical Editor: Michelle Krazniak

Proofreader: Debbye Butler

Production Editor: Tamilmani Varadharaj

Cover Image: © Keith Clouston/Getty Images

Take dummies with you everywhere you go!

Whether you are excited about e-books, want more from the web, must have your mobile apps, or are swept up in social media, dummies makes everything easier.

Find us online!

dummies.com

Leverage the power

Dummies is the global leader in the reference category and one of the most trusted and highly regarded brands in the world. No longer just focused on books, customers now have access to the dummies content they need in the format they want. Together we'll craft a solution that engages your customers, stands out from the competition, and helps you meet your goals.

Advertising & Sponsorships

Connect with an engaged audience on a powerful multimedia site, and position your message alongside expert how-to content. Dummies.com is a one-stop shop for free, online information and know-how curated by a team of experts.

- Targeted ads
- Video
- Email Marketing
- Microsites
- Sweepstakes sponsorship

20 MILLION PAGE VIEWS EVERY SINGLE MONTH

15 MILLION UNIQUE VISITORS PER MONTH

43% OF ALL VISITORS ACCESS THE SITE VIA THEIR MOBILE DEVICES

700,000 NEWSLETTER SUBSCRIPTIONS TO THE INBOXES OF *300,000* UNIQUE INDIVIDUALS EVERY WEEK

# of dummies

Custom Publishing

Reach a global audience in any language by creating a solution that will differentiate you from competitors, amplify your message, and encourage customers to make a buying decision.

- Apps
- Books
- eBooks
- Video
- Audio
- Webinars

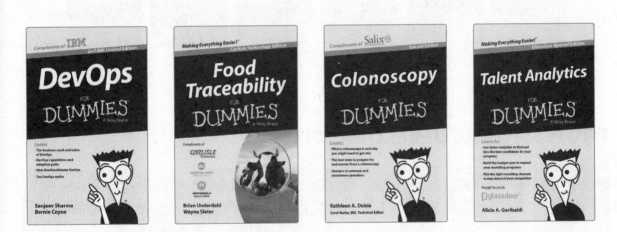

Brand Licensing & Content

Leverage the strength of the world's most popular reference brand to reach new audiences and channels of distribution.

For more information, visit **dummies.com/biz**

PERSONAL ENRICHMENT

Staying Sharp
9781119187790
USA $26.00
CAN $31.99
UK £19.99

Facebook
Carolyn Abram
9781119179030
USA $21.99
CAN $25.99
UK £16.99

Guitar
Mark Phillips
Jon Chappell
9781119293354
USA $24.99
CAN $29.99
UK £17.99

Investing
Eric Tyson, MBA
9781119293347
USA $22.99
CAN $27.99
UK £16.99

Beekeeping
Howland Blackiston
9781119310068
USA $22.99
CAN $27.99
UK £16.99

Digital Photography
Julie Adair King
9781119235606
USA $24.99
CAN $29.99
UK £17.99

Meditation
Stephan Bodian
9781119251163
USA $24.99
CAN $29.99
UK £17.99

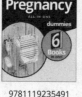

Pregnancy
9781119235491
USA $26.99
CAN $31.99
UK £19.99

Samsung Galaxy S7
Bill Hughes
9781119279952
USA $24.99
CAN $29.99
UK £17.99

iPhone
Edward C. Baig
Bob "Dr. Mac" LeVitus
9781119283133
USA $24.99
CAN $29.99
UK £17.99

Crocheting
Karen Manthey
Susan Brittain
9781119287117
USA $24.99
CAN $29.99
UK £16.99

Nutrition
Carol Ann Rinzler
9781119130246
USA $22.99
CAN $27.99
UK £16.99

PROFESSIONAL DEVELOPMENT

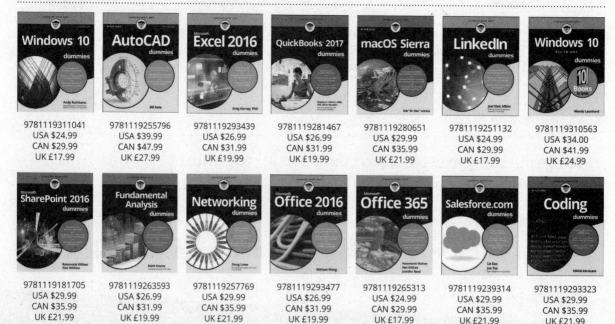

Windows 10
Andy Rathbone
9781119311041
USA $24.99
CAN $29.99
UK £17.99

AutoCAD
Bill Fane
9781119255796
USA $39.99
CAN $47.99
UK £27.99

Excel 2016
Greg Harvey, PhD
9781119293439
USA $26.99
CAN $31.99
UK £19.99

QuickBooks 2017
9781119281467
USA $26.99
CAN $31.99
UK £19.99

macOS Sierra
Bob "Dr. Mac" LeVitus
9781119280651
USA $29.99
CAN $35.99
UK £21.99

LinkedIn
Joel Elad, MBAs
9781119251132
USA $24.99
CAN $29.99
UK £17.99

Windows 10
Woody Leonhard
9781119310563
USA $34.00
CAN $41.99
UK £24.99

SharePoint 2016
Rosemarie Withee
Ken Withee
9781119181705
USA $29.99
CAN $35.99
UK £21.99

Fundamental Analysis
Matt Krantz
9781119263593
USA $26.99
CAN $31.99
UK £19.99

Networking
Doug Lowe
9781119257769
USA $29.99
CAN $35.99
UK £21.99

Office 2016
Wallace Wang
9781119293477
USA $26.99
CAN $31.99
UK £19.99

Office 365
Rosemarie Withee
Ken Withee
Jennifer Reed
9781119265313
USA $24.99
CAN $29.99
UK £17.99

Salesforce.com
Liz Kao
Jon Paz
9781119239314
USA $29.99
CAN $35.99
UK £21.99

Coding
Nikhil Abraham
9781119293323
USA $29.99
CAN $35.99
UK £21.99

dummies.com